The Suitcase

A STORY ABOUT GIVING

JANE G. MEYER

ILLUSTRATED BY

CHIARA PASQUALOTTO

PARACLETE PRESS

BREWSTER, MASSACHUSETTS

2017 First Printing

The Suitcase: A Story About Giving

Text copyright © 2017 by Jane G. Meyer
Illustrations copyright © 2017 by Chiara Pasqualotto

ISBN 978-1-61261-776-3

The Paraclete Press name and logo (dove on cross) are trademarks of Paraclete Press, Inc.

Library of Congress Cataloging-in-Publication Data

Names: Meyer, Jane G., author. | Pasqualotto, Chiara, illustrator.
Title: The suitcase : a story about giving / Jane G. Meyer ;
   illustrated by Chiara Pasqualotto.
Description: Brewster MA : Paraclete Press Inc., 2016. | Summary: Thomas
   packs a suitcase full of items for the needy, inspiring his family to
   visit a homeless shelter.
Identifiers: LCCN 2016033669 | ISBN 9781612617763 (100% matte coated text)
Subjects: | CYAC: Generosity--Fiction. | Family life--Fiction. | Christian
   life--Fiction.
Classification: LCC PZ7.M5716 Su 2016 | DDC [E]--dc23
LC record available at https://lccn.loc.gov/2016033669

10 9 8 7 6 5 4 3 2 1

Published by Paraclete Press
Brewster, Massachusetts
www.paracletepress.com

Printed in the United States of America

The Suitcase

He was maybe just a little bit different, this child named Thomas. He loved to spin in wobbly circles for hours while reciting the alphabet.

Every morning he would interview his pet goat, Greta, about her diet. Did she eat enough grass and weeds and wildflowers the day before? Did she find the mushed carrots and beets delectable? Might she want another taste of his little sister's socks?

And after lunch he would line up all of his blocks—one after another—along the floor. They would stretch from his room down the hallway, through the family room, out the back door and down the steps, across the patio, and finally they would run out when he reached the garden path that led to his favorite bench in the back.

One Sunday, after returning from church, Thomas was being his typical unusual self, chattering and wandering through the yard, and in and out of the house; he even made a trip to the chicken coop.

But when he showed up for dinner with a suitcase in hand, well, that was new. Up popped little invisible question marks over everyone's heads. Over Ava's head. Over Mama's head. Over Daddy's head. Over Charlotte's head. There was even a question mark right above Sparky's head.

"Where are you off to?" Mama asked.
"To the Kingdom of Heaven," Thomas said very matter-of-factly.
There was a nice long pause.

"You know how to
get there?" little Ava
finally asked.

"Well, I've been making a list for a good long time," Thomas said, "and I think I finally know everything I need to bring. So I'm going," he said firmly.

"Come and show us what you've packed," said his daddy. "Because if you're going, I'm coming too."

Thomas tugged his suitcase over to the big round table. Dishes were pushed aside, glasses were placed on the counter, and the big pot of spaghetti went back onto the stove.

He clicked open the locks and pulled the lid wide for everyone to see. On top was a crumpled list.

"See, I got applesauce and a spoon, to feed the hungry."

"And I got an extra jacket, to give clothes to a kid with nothing to wear."

"And I've been saving all of my chore money for three months, and there's seven dollars and thirty-seven cents saved up, which is more than a lot, and I'm gonna give it to someone who needs something." Thomas shook the coin purse and grinned.

"And here's a platter, so I can be a good servant—serve food, or bring folks things when they're sick. And I've got my little book that's full of prayers, so I can pray for the whole wide world."

"And I had to look hard to find this, Mama. It's a mustard seed. I'm bringing this along to plant when I get there. It grows into a gigantic bush that's full of faith!"

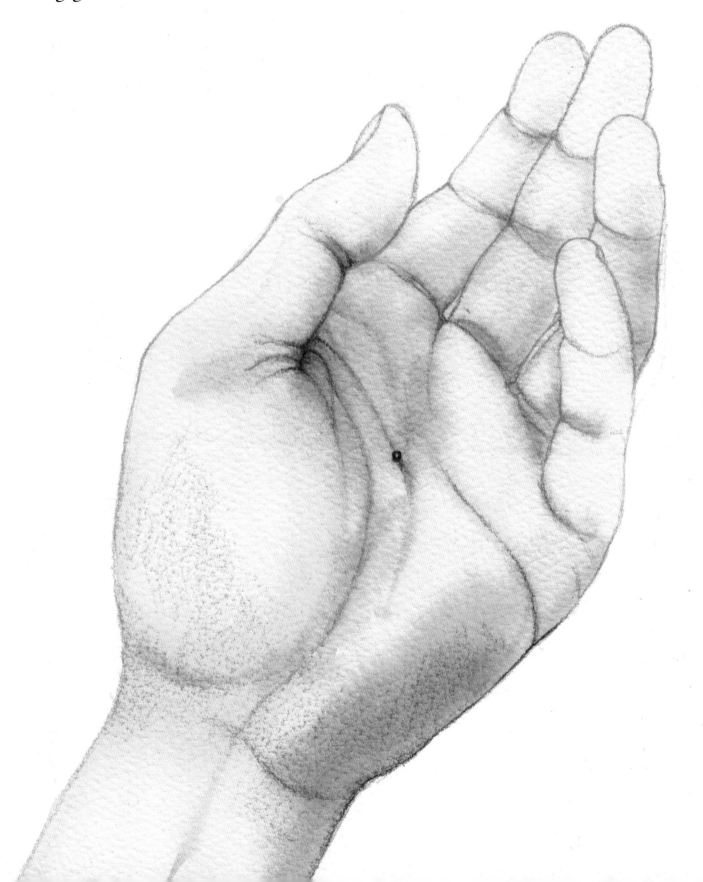

"And I brought some tape, because sometimes I just talk too much and it's important to listen. I wrote that here." Everyone looked at the list, then they looked at each other and smiled. Thomas *was* a bit of a talker.

"And I got this old tablecloth, Mama. I hope you don't mind. It's for entertaining angels. You never know when you might need to get them a drink, or sit with them, or something."

"And I got a bar of soap, so I'm clean. And a hammer, to build things with—like a boat—and Charlotte gave me this pearl a long while ago. She said she didn't need it. It's in case I meet that merchant."

Daddy reached into the suitcase and pulled out a trowel.
"Oh, that's to dig up the Hidden Treasure. I'm sure there'll be some along the way."

There was another long pause. Daddy looked at Mama, and Thomas looked at Ava. Ava looked at Daddy and Charlotte looked at the suitcase and Mama looked at her hands. Mama looked at her hands for a good long time. And then Sparky barked, and everyone laughed, and Thomas asked, "So, can I go now?"

Daddy got up from the table while Mama helped Thomas place the things back in the suitcase and close it. "I just can't think of a reason why we shouldn't all pack!" he said with a grin. "Thomas, whether you know it or not, you are smack dab already in the Kingdom of Heaven."

"Really?" Thomas looked amazed.

"Yep, your good and giving heart shows that you have already walked through that gate."

"So I don't need all this?" Thomas asked, looking puzzled.

"Even though you may be there, Thomas, lots of people have never heard of this place—and they don't know how to take such an amazing journey—so I think we should leave this pot of spaghetti for later." Mama nodded, went into the kitchen and turned off the burner under the pot.

"And we should head out right now."

"To do what?" Charlotte asked.

"To tell the others!" Ava said excitedly.

And that's exactly what they did…

The END

A Resource for Grown-Ups

Zeal and excitement are a part of every child. And sometimes, a child can see through all of the stuff and clutter of this life and get straight to the most important charge we have as Christians: to pack our suitcases and head out to share the Kingdom of Heaven! Be careful not to squelch a young child's enthusiasm to put into practice the words of Christ: feed and clothe the poor, help the needy, and love your neighbor. There is nothing worse than to be a little person filled with a big idea, and be told, *Sorry, honey, not today. Why don't you just go and play. . . .*

Here are a few ideas to consider for when your child comes to the dinner table with a suitcase packed and ready to go. Remember, when help is given in person in a slow and deliberate manner—when the giver stops to really see the receiver and learn his or her name and story, like Christ did—it is life-changing for the giver and the receiver. Writing a check is lovely, but it's relationships that heal and help us grow.

- There are homeless ministries and soup kitchens in almost every community. Some are willing to have folks of all ages come and help. This is a wonderful way for an entire family to serve those in need.
- Prepare music, or cards, or treats as a family, then bring them on a visit to a home for the elderly.
- Find someone who struggles with seeing or reading, to whom your child can offer to read on a regular basis.
- Talk with your child about kids at school. Identify one who is often left out of activities and invite that child over to play.
- Contact your church community and find out if there is an appropriate person who can't travel outside their home, for whom your child could do errands or yard work, or could visit.
- Do you have a relative who could use a listening ear? Do you perhaps need to re-forge your bond first? A child's love is often the best icebreaker when family tensions have deep roots.
- Volunteer as a family at the local food bank and help stock their shelves and distribute food to the needy.
- Pack up small bags of necessities to give to those living on the street. Include a travel-sized toothbrush, wipes, and toothpaste, along with new socks, lip balm, a small icon or prayer card, and a coupon to a local food establishment. Keep them in your car for when you come across someone in need.
- Invite a friend or neighbor to join your family at a natural setting and together discover the beauty that God has put there for us to enjoy.
- Above all, pray—pray alone, and pray as a family—and seek ways to fill up your hearts with Christ's unending love.

How does God's love abide in anyone who has the world's goods and sees a brother or sister in need and yet refuses help? Little children, let us love, not in word or speech, but in truth and action.
(1 John 3:17–18 NRSV)

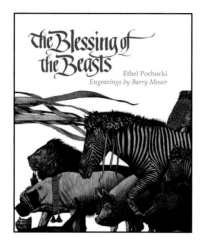

The Blessing of the Beasts
by Ethel Pochocki, Illustrated by Barry Moser

$15.99 | 978-1-61261-582-0 | Paperback

Francesca, a roach, and Martin, a skunk, originally met in a trash can a while back: He'd startled her by rising from the garbage, wearing a cap of coleslaw and a mustache of yogurt. Francesca had always been warned about churches. They were too clean, barren of food, and they were dangerous. As the St. Francis Blessing of the Animals approaches, Francesca wants to go, but Martin warns her against it: "I don't think that we are meant to be included, Francesca. It's for the respectables, the cute and cuddlies. We are outcasts. They'll never let us in. Can't you just hear the humans shrieking as we walk down the aisle? They'd be fainting left and right." Kids and adults alike will treasure this story, with its illustrations by the acclaimed Barry Moser, about how all of God's creation has value, purpose, and blessing.

ETHEL POCHOCKI was the author of several other books for children and adults, including *Once Upon a Time Saints*. BARRY MOSER is one of the most acclaimed illustrators alive today.

Butterflies Under our Hats
by Sandy Eisenberg Sasso, Illustrated by Joani Keller Rothenberg

$15.99 | 978-1-61261-583-7 | Paperback

Folklore has been used throughout history to teach and inspire—this new release in paperback will do just that. Inspired by a Jewish folktale, this charming original story begins: Once there was a town called Chelm where there was no luck. If something could go wrong, it did. The roofs of the houses always leaked. The sidewalks were cracked. The gardens grew only weeds. Nothing was ever right. But just wait and find hope with best-selling author Sandy Eisenberg Sasso (nearly 500,000 copies of her books are in print).

SANDY EISENBERG SASSO is the best-selling author of *In God's Name*, *God's Paintbrush*, *Creation's First Light*, and other books. JOANI ROTHENBERG is the illustrator of several children's books. She lives in Indianapolis.

IMAGES
of America

WELLS FARGO

IMAGES
of America

WELLS FARGO

Dr. Robert J. Chandler

ARCADIA
PUBLISHING

Published by Arcadia Publishing
Charleston SC, Chicago IL, Portsmouth NH, San Francisco CA

Printed in the United States of America

Library of Congress Catalog Card Number: 2006923108

For all general information contact Arcadia Publishing at:
Telephone 843-853-2070
Fax 843-853-0044
E-mail sales@arcadiapublishing.com
For customer service and orders:
Toll-Free 1-888-313-2665

Visit us on the Internet at www.arcadiapublishing.com

To Sue

CONTENTS

ACKNOWLEDGMENTS

Almost 30 years ago, Wells Fargo bankers Bob Livingston of Sacramento and Jack Weaver of Woodland mentored this greenhorn on the intricacies of Wells Fargo history. Furthermore, they showed how much fun it could be.

John Poultney, Jaquelin Pelzer, and Christine Talbot of Arcadia Publishing, and Bev Smith of Wells Fargo pushed this project along. Additionally, Bev and Bill Saner read several drafts. Archivist Christy Johnson speedily retrieved treasures hidden behind a three-foot-thick armored vault door. Rebecca Rubin, Bill Sander, and John Keibel formed a photographic scan team to ready 210 prime illustrations. All have my thanks.

Unless noted, all photographs are in possession of Wells Fargo or the author.

INTRODUCTION

Wells Fargo is a modern, worldwide financial services company with a legendary name out of the Old West. In 1852, Wells Fargo opened with a half-dozen employees in San Francisco. Today, it is the city's largest private employer, with 8,000 employees. Over the last century and a half, Wells Fargo has grown and evolved. The procedures and businesses of today are not those of California's gold-rush era. Yet, an iconographic 19th-century stagecoach ties together that long history. Wells Fargo's vermillion-and-straw Concord coach carries values set in the past through the present and into the future.

In 1849, more than prospective red-shirted miners looked to distant California gold fields. In New York City, Henry Wells and William George Fargo dreamed of riches, too. First, on March 18, 1850, they consolidated three regional New York express companies into the American Express Company, becoming president and vice president respectively. Then Wells and Fargo gazed west. On March 18, 1852, they organized Wells, Fargo & Company to serve the Pacific coast.

New markets mandated new methods for conducting business. In the Atlantic states, American Express rapidly carried money and valuables, the core of the express business. In California, frontier conditions led Wells Fargo additionally to offer banking and fast delivery of letters. When the first Wells Fargoans stepped ashore in June 1852, they discovered a lack of ethics in San Francisco commerce. The craze to get ahead in business emulated Darwin's theory of evolution; "Survival of the fittest" was the slogan.

Wells Fargo was one firm that held to values. "We are a company that does business on the fair and square," its corporate secretary wrote in 1869. "We do not propose to take advantage of anybody; we will make a good bargain whenever we can, and get what we can; but as to ever intending to take advantage of the government or anybody else, we do not propose to do it."

In the 1850s and 1860s, Wells Fargo grew with the mining economy, expanding throughout California and heading north to Oregon, Washington, and British Columbia and east to Nevada, Idaho, Montana, Utah, Montana, Colorado, and Arizona. Letter delivery led Wells Fargo into overland stagecoaching and the pony express. Beginning in 1857, the affiliated Overland Mail Company received U.S. government contracts to carry mail between the Missouri River and California. Wells Fargo accepted this opportunity to expand its area of service eastward.

In 1888, Wells, Fargo & Company's Express went "ocean to ocean," with a through rail line to the Atlantic and "over the sea" to Europe and Asia. Refrigerated railcars enhanced the American diet with fresh produce and seafood. Wells Fargo money orders paid for packages sent everywhere.

Change came in 1905, when railroad magnate Edward H. Harriman, who controlled Wells Fargo, separated its two major businesses and moved Wells Fargo & Company Express to New York. As extensive as it was, Wells Fargo would find that this express track led nowhere. During World War I, the federal government consolidated the domestic express business. As a result, in 1918, a total of 10,000 Wells Fargo offices joined American Railway Express. Only a small Cuban-and-Mexican express business remained under the Wells Fargo name.

Banking enabled Wells Fargo to evolve into the financial powerhouse it is today. Beginning in the 1890s, Wells Fargo closed or sold its interstate banks in Nevada, New York, Oregon, and Utah, and in 1905, at Harriman's urging, Wells, Fargo & Company's Bank joined its San Francisco neighbor, the Nevada National Bank. Growth continued through the merger. In 1924, Wells Fargo Bank and Union Trust Company began operating under a California banking charter. Marriage with American Trust Company and its retail bank network followed in 1960.

As Wells Fargo clustered around the San Francisco Bay area, the remainder of the huge state of California called. Its first Southern California branch opened in December 1967. In 1968, a national bank holding company emblazoned with the historic 1852 name of Wells Fargo & Company started a continental advance through nonbanking subsidiaries.

A merger with The Crocker Bank in 1986 doubled Wells Fargo's size. Consolidations with First Interstate in 1996 and with Norwest in 1998 made Wells Fargo an interstate bank in 23 states, with financial and mortgage services offered nationally and internationally. Through each merger, Wells Fargo's name emerged for the future.

PAST PRESIDENTS

WELLS, FARGO & COMPANY, BANKING AND EXPRESS

1852–1853	Edwin B. Morgan
1853–1866	Danford N. Barney
1866–1868	Louis McLane
1868–1870	Ashbel H. Barney
1870–1872	William G. Fargo
1872–1892	Lloyd Tevis
1892–1901	John J. Valentine
1902–1905	Dudley Evans

WELLS FARGO & COMPANY EXPRESS
(POST 1918, CUBA, MEXICO, AND ARMORED CAR BUSINESS)

1905–1910	Dudley Evans
1910–1911	William Sproule
1911–1922	Burns D. Caldwell
1922–1925	Davis G. Mellor
1925–1955	Elmer Jones
1956–1960	R. T. Reed
1960–1963	Howard L. Clark
1963–1964	R. D. Beals
1964–1967	James A. Henderson

WELLS FARGO BANK

1905–1920	Isaias W. Hellman
1920	I. W. Hellman II
1920–1935	Frederick L. Lipman
1935–1943	Robert B. Motherwell II
1943–1960	I. W. Hellman III
1960–1964	Ransom M. Cook
1964–1966	H. Stephen Chase
1966–1979	Richard P. Cooley, CEO 1979–1982
1979–1984	Carl E. Reichardt, CEO 1982–1994
1984–1994	Paul Hazen, CEO 1995–1998
1995–1997	William F. Zuendt
1997–1998	Paul Hazen
1998	Rodney L. Jacobs
1998–2005	Richard M. Kovacevich, CEO 1998–present
2005	John G. Stumpf

"CEO" is a modern title that outranks "President." At times, the chief executive officer is also president.

One

FOUNDING A COMPANY

Forming a business is the easy part; profitability and survival are more difficult. When the rush to California began in 1849, the express business in the eastern United States was only 10 years old. Its specialty of rapidly transporting money made it labor intensive and dependant upon the integrity of numerous employees.

Gold, though, exerted a powerful influence, and on November 8, 1849, nine-year-old Adams & Company became the first of the prominent eastern express companies to offer Californians its services. In addition to delivering letters, Adams & Company also served as a banker, buying and selling gold dust—or forwarding it to the Philadelphia mint to be coined—and selling drafts payable in the East.

American Express Company, a combination of smaller expresses run by Henry Wells, John Butterfield, and William G. Fargo, did not open for business until March 18, 1850. As the new firm struggled to gain momentum, a personality clash between Butterfield and Fargo prevented it from venturing west into unknown areas.

On March 18, 1852, Wells, Fargo, and friends risked heading for Pacific shores, and their Wells, Fargo & Company opened for business on July 13, 1852, in San Francisco and Sacramento. In the tumultuous California economy, Wells Fargo went up against the larger, aggressive, and entrenched Page, Bacon & Company, which offered banking services, and Adams & Company, which offered both banking and express services. Yet, in 1855, dishonest banking practices doomed Page, Bacon & Company and Adams & Company. Wells Fargo's bank flourished, and its express services became dominant. The express successors to Adams & Company never had the vigor of their parent. Wells, Fargo & Company's Express operated through ocean and river steamers, stagecoaches, and, beginning in 1856, through the Sacramento Valley Railroad.

In December 1855, Louis McLane (1819–1905) assured the growth of Wells, Fargo & Company. McLane's service in the U.S. Navy trained him well. Under him, Wells Fargo increased its efficiency and kept to legitimate businesses.

In 1863, William G. Fargo and Wells Fargo president Danford N. Barney traveled dustily by overland stagecoach to California. There they worked with the San Francisco-owned Sacramento Valley Railroad and its affiliates to build the first transcontinental railroad over the Sierra Nevada via Placerville. In the meantime, the Central Pacific Railroad, a Sacramento firm headed by merchant Leland Stanford, laid Sierra-bound track by way of Dutch Flat and Auburn.

Two years later, a visiting eastern journalist remarked that Wells Fargo was "the omnipresent, universal business agent" of the West. How did Wells Fargo do it? It provided good service and treated its customers well. In 1888, Wells Fargo wrote down long-established procedures in its instructions to agents: "The most polite and gentlemanly treatment of all customers, however insignificant their business, is insisted upon. Proper respect must be shown to all—let them be men, women or children, rich or poor, white or black—it must not be forgotten that the Company is dependent on these same people for its business."

On March 18, 1852, a purposeful group of men gathered in New York City's elegant Astor House Hotel. American Express president Henry Wells and secretary William G. Fargo would organize a new joint-stock company to engage in business on the far off Pacific coast. It would carry their names, Wells, Fargo & Company.

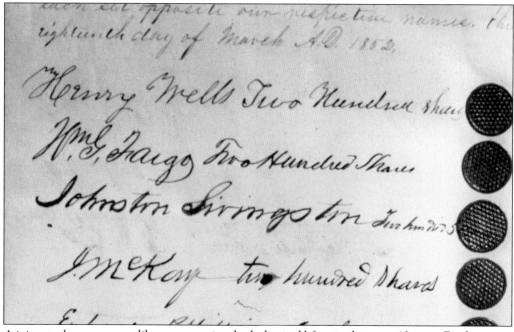

A joint-stock company, unlike a corporation, had a limited life—in this case, 10 years. Furthermore, it did not have corporate legal standing as a "person," making its shareholders individually liable for its debts, as well as eligible to share its profits. In spite of such risk, in 1859, Wells Fargo had 130 shareholders, and 12 percent of them were women.

Henry Wells

In the 1840s, Henry Wells (1805–1878), a gregarious giant of a man, pioneered early expressing, cheap mail delivery, and commercial telegraph lines. The achievement of his life, though, was Wells College for women, opened in 1868 in Aurora, New York.

William George Fargo (1818–1881) led a public life. He followed Henry Wells as president of American Express, which Fargo headed from 1868 to 1881; ran the City of Buffalo, New York, as mayor during the Civil War; and acted as a director of the Northern Pacific Railroad. Through that connection, in 1872, Fargo helped found Norwest, Wells Fargo's 1998 merger partner, and in 1871, he gave his name to Fargo, North Dakota.

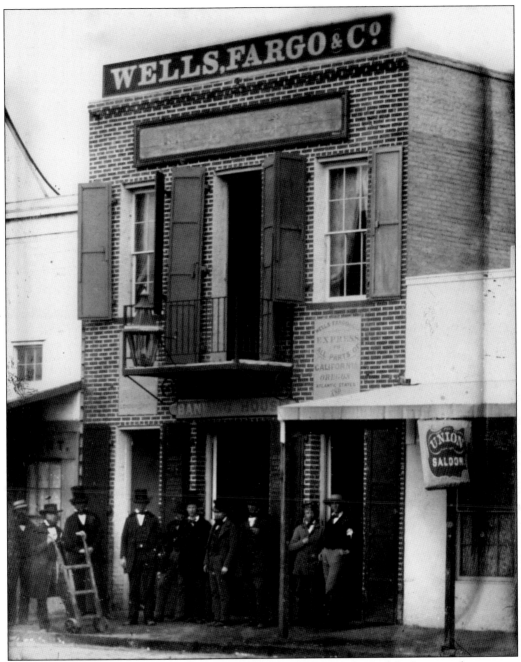

In late June 1852, a steamer deposited Wells Fargo expressman Samuel P. Carter in boomtown San Francisco. On July 13, 1852, Carter and banker Reuben W. Washburn opened for business at 424 Montgomery Street, a few feet from Wells Fargo Bank's current headquarters, at 420 on the same street.

Reuben W. Washburn, Wells Fargo's first banker, owned the stock certificate pictured here, entitling him to "all the rights" of the association. Recognizing Wells Fargo's closeness to American Express, the printers used the same stock certificate design but reversed the direction of the railroad.

A financial panic on February 23, 1855, or "Black Friday," saw thousands of customers besieging banks and demanding money. The state's two largest banks, Page, Bacon & Company and Adams & Company, headquartered in the Parrott Building, came crashing down. Later that year, marking its ascendancy, Wells Fargo moved into the vacated space. Wells Fargo would retain this 62-foot Montgomery Street frontage until 1876.

In Wells Fargo's gas-lit banking office, as wood engraver Durbin Van Vleck illustrated, two miners stand by the huge bullion scale, offering bags of gold dust to be weighed. Pictured here, the paying teller counts out $700 in double eagles for two elegantly dressed women about to begin shopping along fashionable Montgomery Street. Down the counter, a bank officer informs a nattily dressed customer that his loan until the next semi-monthly Steamer Day will be at two percent a month—2006 credit card rates. Two others stand discussing the latest speculative Nevada silver stocks.

To the right of the banking room, customers entered Wells Fargo's express department from Montgomery Street. Here they dropped off or picked up packages and letters to and from the interior of California or the Atlantic states. By 4:25 p.m., the river steamers would have departed, and the office would have been relatively calm.

Wells Fargo's bookkeepers occupied a well-lit office facing the courtyard. Two bookkeepers sitting on high stools enter accounts in ledgers resting on high, slanted desks. Across the way, a top-hatted clerk checks to see whether Miss Susan received the Wells Fargo draft to bring her out to California to marry the lucky gentleman carrying a California gold-quartz-headed cane.

The *Orizaba* was one of many ships that ran up and down the coast between San Diego and Victoria, British Columbia, carrying Wells Fargo messengers and its express cargo. (Courtesy of the Book Club of California, San Francisco.)

Louis McLane, the scion of a proud Baltimore family, learned discipline, daring, and doing in the U.S. Navy. General Agent McLane demanded responsibility. He quickly appointed two reporting superintendents—one for banking, the other for express—and picked traveling-route agents to inspect all offices. In the fall of 1856, McLane printed the first employee instructions of any California express.

Louis McLane

From December 1865 until February 1869, Wells Fargo efficiently handled all freight for the Pacific Mail Steamship Company. About 1:00 p.m. on Monday, April 16, 1866, a Wells Fargo porter standing in the Parrott Building courtyard began prying off the top of a large wooden box that had arrived by the last steamer. A huge explosion erupted in flame and brown smoke, shooting up debris to 400 feet. This wrecked building stood on the courtyard's far side. Among the dozen dead were Samuel Knight, superintendent of Wells Fargo's banking department, and his predecessor, assayer Gerritt W. Bell. The unknown chemical was nitroglycerin.

Sometimes Wells Fargo guessed wrong. In 1861, Wells Fargo allowed its Portland agent E. W. Tracy to run his own express to western Idaho. In 1862, Wells Fargo bought out Tracy, but in spring 1863, their rivalry spread to the Boise Basin. Wells Fargo entered the unknown territory, quickly came to its senses, and withdrew after three weeks. In August 1863, Tracy's Express entered the Boise Basin. Wells Fargo followed on October 1, and within six weeks, again purchased Tracy's Express. A resounding welcome greeted Wells Fargo at Silver City. (Courtesy Idaho Historical Society, Boise.)

High Civil War casualties overwhelmed the army's ability to care for sick and wounded soldiers, and, in 1861, civilians organized the United States Sanitary Commission, a predecessor to the Red Cross. In December 1864, citizens of Arcata auctioned off this "National Sanitary Cake" state by state, raising $700, and sent the cake to neighboring Eureka. Its auction added another $1,000. From 1862 through 1865, Californians raised one-fourth of the $5 million collected, and Wells Fargo brought the funds free of charge to San Francisco.

"This steamer is the wonder of the age," a watchman aboard the huge *Great Eastern*, docked in New York City, declared. During the Paris World's Fair in 1867, prominent San Francisco and New York merchant William T. Coleman handled horses, while Wells Fargo booked passengers.

The fast steamer *Antelope* represented Wells Fargo's service on California's rivers. Wells Fargo cargoes of Nevada silver bricks, often weighing together a ton and a half, posed problems. Early in 1863, the California Steam Navigation Company shored up a stateroom on the *Antelope* to prevent the bars from crashing through the deck.

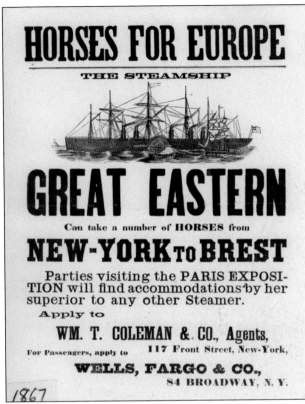

HORSES FOR EUROPE

THE STEAMSHIP

GREAT EASTERN

Can take a number of **HORSES** from

NEW-YORK TO BREST

Parties visiting the PARIS EXPOSI-
TION will find accommodations by her
superior to any other Steamer.

Apply to

WM. T. COLEMAN & CO., Agents,

For Passengers, apply to   **117 Front Street, New-York,**

WELLS, FARGO & CO.,

84 BROADWAY, N. Y.

1867

William M. Robison, active in the 1850s African American civil rights movement, gained praise as a Wells Fargo wagon driver around Stockton. In the river port town of Sacramento, Wells Fargoan London Luff distributed packages in 1856 and 1857. Californians hungered for news, and Luff was the first to bring it. "He always has upon our table the latest dates at the earliest moments," remarked the *Sacramento Union*. (Courtesy of the Haggin Museum, Stockton, California.)

On one of the few a restful days, a Wells Fargo agent could lean back in his chair, his wife beside him, and invite customers inside. The arched sign on the right advertises that the agent pictured here would buy gold dust.

20

Two

GOLD RUSH FINANCE
BANKING FOR THOSE
ON THE MOVE

"We'd never think of settling here for life," a prominent merchant's wife declared in 1848, while an ordinary miner's wife wrote in 1856, "We will be back there [in Illinois] as soon as we get as much money as will settle us down comfortable and nice." Not until the 1860s did sentiment swing to staying in the West.

Miners and merchants rushed from claim to claim, as word constantly came of newfound strikes of inestimable riches just over the next ridge. Letters from home came to wherever the recipient had moved, while expressmen carried away replies and money.

In a gold rush town, constant activity in and out of a building signified that it was a Wells Fargo office. Auburn agent John Q. Jackson attended to customers all day and wrote business letters between busy times.

Twenty years after the rush, gold still came out of the hills. In 1876, for instance, Wells Fargo agent Henry Sevening in Columbia sent down about 3,700 ounces of pure gold, gaining a two percent profit on the transactions. Additionally, as town banker, he made small loans of $2.50 to $40 to residents. For his Chinese customers, Sevening accepted pistols, watches, specimens, and gold jewelry as collateral for sums from $3 to $10.

Gold coin weighed three and a half pounds per $1,000. Carrying large sums became cumbersome and tempting to robbers. Checks and other financial paper became the solution. Wells Fargo drafts were safer, lighter in weight, much more convenient, and could be redeemed anywhere.

Circulating types of money, though, taxed Wells Fargo's ingenuity. Today the dollar has one value. During the 1860s and 1870s, Californians handled three differently valued U.S. moneys: gold, silver, and paper. Naturally, gold-producing California remained on a gold standard. In 1861, during the Civil War, the federal government uncoupled paper money from gold, and the 1870s brought a glut of silver. Only in 1879 did all U.S. moneys—gold, silver, and paper—return to the same value.

On January 24, 1848, James Marshall followed a hunch to use the water ditch that powered the saw in John Sutter's lumber mill as a giant sluice box. The rushing waters cleared debris to reveal shining gold in bedrock cracks. This place, now known as the Marshall Gold Rush Discovery Site, has a tale of freedom in its history. In 1942, the state purchased the land from the Monroe family, whose California ancestor Nancy Gooch arrived as a slave in 1849. Freed by the state constitution, she quickly purchased son Andrew and daughter-in-law Sarah Monroe out of Missouri slavery, proving that gold could provide personal as well as financial freedom.

A miner with a gold pan became the symbol of the gold rush. Artist Charles Nahl drew this happy gold seeker in 1854. Casually picking up money from the ground, as it were, amazed many.

The Panic of 1837, when the money issued by hundreds of state banks became worthless, remained fixed in the minds of the framers of California's 1849 constitution. A huge percent of eastern money was counterfeit, and the Suffolk Bank of Boston undertook to check all money circulating in its area. The note pictured here failed all tests.

A golden fortune awaited forty-niners, but raw gold was neither money nor legal tender. On September 9, 1848, $16 a troy ounce became the fixed price for gold dust, while pure gold at the mint brought $20.67. Beginning in 1849, San Franciscans melted gold to make their own coins, which were valued at the mint price. In 1851, the U.S. government only legally recognized two-and-a-half-ounce $50 gold pieces, such as the one pictured here.

Miners quickly and cooperatively engaged in huge civil-engineering projects, such as damming and diverting rivers to get at rich gravels; bringing water from miles away; and using strong jets of water to blast away hillsides. Here, an undershot flutter wheel on the fast-flowing Tuolumne River raises water to wash gold flakes out of surrounding gravel and black iron sand.

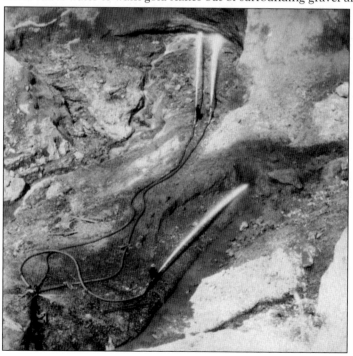

In 1866, photographer Alfred A. Hart captured the ecological disaster wrought by hydraulic mining, the most inexpensive placer method developed to separate gold from tons of gravel. The devastation shown here may be seen today at the rest stop on Interstate 80 at Gold Run, in Placer County. Mud and rock fouled river channels, leading to widespread flooding of fertile downstream farmlands. In 1884, in an early action by the courts, a federal judge protected the environment by ordering miners to impound tailings.

In 1865, fortunate El Dorado County miners discovered a glorious 14-pound mass of crystalline gold. It rests on three gold bars, which were cast and assayed by, from left to right, John G. Kellogg, John Hewston & Company; Henry Hentsch and Francis Berton; and August P. Molitor. Melting gold dust into bars cleaned and concentrated it, making it easier to transport. Stampings provided exact information as to weight, purity, and value. Now known as the Fricot Nugget, it greets visitors to the State of California's mineral collection at the Mariposa County Fair Grounds.

Wells Fargo agents purchased and shipped gold dust. Auburn, the county seat of Placer County, served as a crossroads for gold coming from Yankee Jim's, Iowa Hill, Michigan Bluff, and Rattlesnake Bar. This 1857 illustration shows a stagecoach crammed with gold-dust sellers heads for the Wells Fargo office, which still stands in the island.

In 1852, Wells Fargo placed 20-year-old John Quincy Jackson in charge of a large express office and banking house. "What I have to do is quite confining," Jackson wrote to his brother, "staying in my office all day till ten at night—buying dust, forwarding and receiving packages of every kind, from and to everywhere—[and] filling out drafts for the Eastern Mails in all sorts of sums, from $50 to $1,000."

Monthly, Auburn agent John Q. Jackson sent down to San Francisco some $200,000 worth of gold dust, weighing perhaps 750 pounds. Shipments were "frequently 100 to 150 pounds—about as much as one likes to shoulder to and from the stages," he observed. Was he worried about security? Not at all. "As a friend, counselor, and safe guard," Jackson owned a "devoted" 128-pound bull mastiff.

A Wells Fargo agent's authority came through a paper-agency appointment, not with a badge. Agents were not law officers. Wells Fargo insisted that the appointment "must be conspicuously posted in the Office." The one seen here is from 1884 and defines the powers and duties of Portland, Oregon, agent Eugene Shelby.

This photograph shows a set of gold scales as in the left front counter of J. Q. Jackson's office. Edward Howard and David Davis of Boston made precision balance scales, which their catalogue claimed were "acknowledged as the standards throughout California." They guaranteed that their 40-year old patented design would weigh every grain of gold a miner presented, and 480 grains made a troy ounce.

Wells Fargo's Columbia office is easily recognizable. In 1945, Wells Fargo Bank presented it to the new state park. Wells Fargo set rules for its Columbia agent in 1857, and they applied to all its gold-buyers. The rules stated, "Pay no more for dust than it is worth, nor pay less. This is the only true motto to do any kind of business on."

Much of the gold Wells Fargo carried down from the mines went into U.S. gold coins. In 1856, this illustration appeared in James Mason Hutchings's *California Magazine*. By means of the large wheel, the coiner dropped a blank on the lower die as the hydraulic press brought down the upper die to squeeze out a perfect coin.

ADJUSTING ROOM.

The mint pioneered the employment of women. Here in the Adjusting Room, women weigh new coin blanks to make certain they are within allowed tolerances. The mint melted those too light and filed down blanks too heavy. When the new mint at Fifth and Mission Streets, now a museum, opened in 1875, women also ran the hydraulic coining presses.

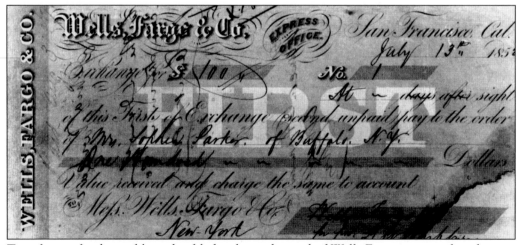

Transferring funds quickly and safely has been the goal of Wells Fargo since its founding, as shown by its first eastern draft, dated July 13, 1852. Filled out in duplicate—and, if needed, triplicate—each copy of a bill of exchange sailed on a different steamship. Wells Fargo would pay the first to arrive; the other copies would become void.

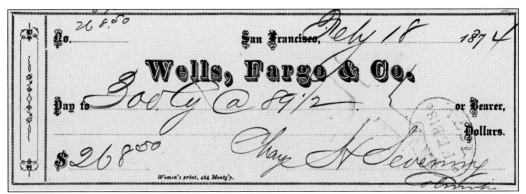

When Southern rebels rejoiced over battlefield victories, government greenbacks lost value. California merchants demanded that bills be paid in gold coin, and they took paper money only at its daily equivalent to gold. On February 18, 1874, the date of the check shown here, greenbacks were worth 89.5¢. A Wells Fargo banker helped organize the Women's Cooperative Printing Union, which offered new occupational opportunities for women. Note the printmark at bottom center: "Women's print, 424 Montg'y."

Beginning in 1873, silver glutted the world market, soon falling to 95¢ on the gold dollar. Levi Strauss & Company, "manufacturers of the celebrated patent riveted denim pants," boldly informed customers in red ink which money it would receive. Banks kept accounts in three U.S. moneys—gold, silver, and greenbacks—all of which circulated at different values. The billhead shown here exhibits the distinctive lettering style of African American lithographer Grafton Tyler Brown.

Even in the most isolated regions of the West, people expected to find Wells Fargo. In this photograph, a closed-in mud wagon pulls up on a cool day in front of the Bear River Hotel, where the Wells Fargo sign is almost as large as the office.

Three

RAPID LETTER DELIVERY

"I have not received any letters from you for two months," a gold rush miner wrote his wife. "I hardly know what to think." Miners and merchants yearned for word from home, and Wells Fargo's letter service became "a necessity on this coast," as Wells Fargo said.

Inflated gold rush costs and long, slow communications hampered the quality of the U.S. Postal Service. Beginning in 1849, private express companies sprang up in California to carry letters to and from the mines. There were usually from one to several men in a firm, and they charged up to $2 in addition to 40¢ U.S. postage on letters arriving from the East.

From 1849 to 1869, side-wheel steamers regularly carried mail between San Francisco and New York. When steamer day came around, which was twice a month, Wells Fargo handled letters. "I never thought much of the Overland route," a miner muttered from Murphys (Calaveras County) in 1862, "the Steamer Line was a sure shot."

Overland stagecoaches began competing with oceangoing steamers in September 1858. Not only did horsepower cut two days or more off of the time taken by steam power, but frequency of deliveries increased from 2 times a month by sea to 8 times by land, and then in 1861, to 26 times monthly. Delivering letters overland under contract with the U.S. government drew Wells Fargo into overland stagecoaching and the pony express.

On February 15, 1855, the federal government began enforcing an 1852 law that allowed express companies to carry letters, but only if enclosed in envelopes that had prepaid printed U.S. postage. The post office never touched these letters, and the government therefore placed an onerous burden upon a public that valued efficiency.

The continued express competition benefited residents through declining fees. In mid-August 1855, the Pacific Express Company dropped its letter charge to 10¢, including the 3¢ U.S. postage cost, and Wells Fargo followed suit. Wells Fargo's rivalry with the short-lived Pacific Union Express in July 1868 brought about a uniform express charge of 5¢ for all letters, which lasted almost 30 years.

Battles for business spurred further efficiency. In August 1855, the Pacific Express began printing its name on government stamped envelopes with the notation that express charges were "paid." This printed device is known as a "frank," and all of the expresses adopted the practice. Wells Fargo, though, added colors to speed routing: black for local mail; red for letters going to the Atlantic states; blue for special expedited service; green for Mexico; and brown for Hawaii. By the 1860s, Wells Fargo carried 75 percent of the mail within California. Businesses used Wells Fargo regularly. It beat the post office: by sorting letters en route, setting up mailboxes, and delivering letters to businesses and homes. "Don't send me any more mail through the Post Office," a man in San Jose wrote in the mid-1850s to a friend in San Francisco, "for it takes a week to get here. Give it to Wells Fargo and I'll get it in 9 hours."

In 1880, the post office attempted to shut down Wells Fargo's Letter Express. The press rallied to the support of a company that "is true as steel and prompt as clockwork," as a Walla Walla, Washington, paper declared in praise. The *San Leandro Journal* reported, "The train which carries the U.S. mail leaves here once a day, each way," and added that "those carrying Wells, Fargo & Co., [leave] four times a day, each way. Letters and packages sent by this service are delivered at residences."

In May 1895, close to 50 years after the gold rush, Wells Fargo discontinued its famed letter express.

The Post Office, corner of Pike and Clay streets.

When the steamer arrived with letters from loved ones in the East, hundreds of anxious Californians waited in front of the post office. In 1849, Alexander Hamilton Todd of Stockton compiled a list of local recipients and picked up their letters in San Francisco. They saved time, and Todd made money and inaugurated the express business in California.

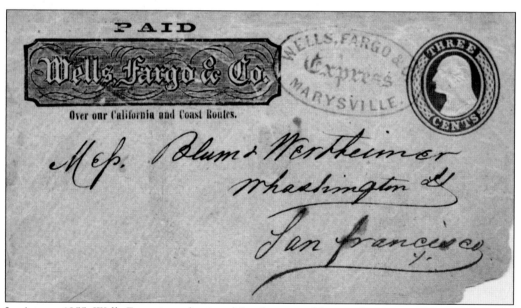

In August 1855, Wells Fargo issued printed franks created by wood engraver Warren C. Butler and using the lettering style from its eastern drafts. Wells Fargo quickly carried the letter pictured here from Marysville to the pioneer San Francisco clothing firm of Leopold Blum and Leopold Wertheimer.

As this early 1890s photograph shows, Wells Fargo's letter box (left) was a central feature of Wells Fargo's Grass Valley office. The large brown ceramic jug on top entices viewers to guess its contents. While two clerks man the counter of the gas-lit room, a "wheelman," as bicyclists were known, stands with his "wheels" next to a hand truck. Near him, rate tables on the front of a stationery cabinet offer easy access, and a framed poster lists offices paying money sent by telegraph. In an etching on the back wall (just left of center), William Fargo, looks down benignly. Samuel P. Dorsey, noted owner of the Idaho-Maryland Mine, ran this Wells Fargo office from 1857 to 1904.

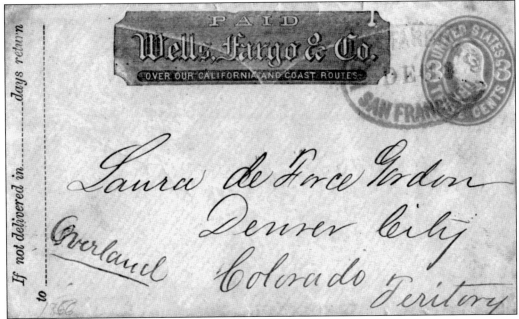

Wells Fargo adopted a new frank design in December 1855, and used it until its letter express ended in May 1895. In December 1866, a Wells Fargo's overland stagecoach delivered an invitation to Denver asking speaker Laura DeForce Gordon to come to California. Eighteen months later, Gordon gave the first speech in the state advocating women's suffrage.

Wells Fargo organized its letters at sea, allowing it to hand them out on arrival, while the post office was still sorting the incoming mail. In the mid-1860s, the wooden 343-foot side-wheel *Golden City* departs San Francisco for Panama, cruising at an economical 10.5 knots.

"While on way up on Pacific side, prepare a careful alphabetical list of all San Francisco Letters in your Bag," Wells Fargo ordered a steamer messenger in 1855. "Then throw Bag Letters and Bag Newspapers to the captain [of our news boat]: Be ready for him so as not to miss him." Horsemen then raced from the North Beach wharf, pictured here in the 1870s, into the city. With Meigg's Wharf in the foreground, the *City of Peking* (built in 1874) sails for China. The tall plume of smoke from the departing steamer shows that coal was a messy fuel.

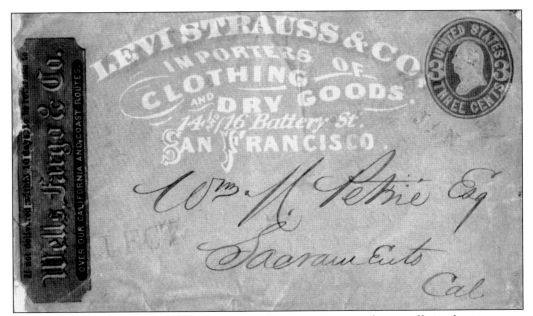

Beginning in the summer of 1859, Freeman & Company's express began offering businessmen, for a penny more, envelopes with lithographed advertising, and Wells Fargo followed. On January 1, 1870, the pioneer blue-jeans maker dispatched this festive cover to a J Street clothing store in Sacramento.

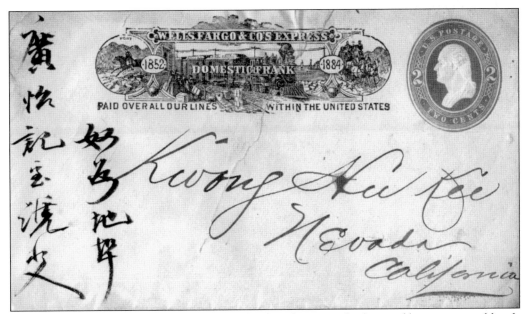

In 1883 and 1884, Wells Fargo used a design showing the ways it had carried letters since gold rush days—by pony express, stagecoach, and railroad. It was, declared its creator, supply officer Aaron Stein, "intended principally to keep Uncle Sam constantly reminded that the letter service of Wells, Fargo & Co. was of no recent and cunningly devised invasion of government prerogative." The letter shown here was sent to a Chinese merchant in Nevada City.

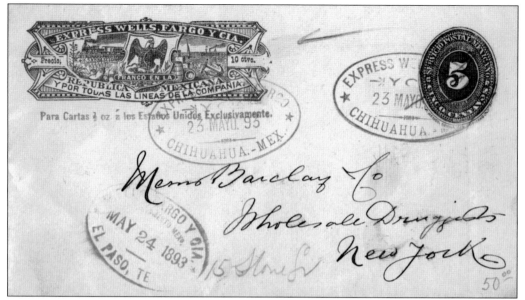

Wells Fargo's first Mexican office opened in 1860 in the coastal port of Guaymas. Along with the expansion of the Mexican railroads in the early 1880s, over 300 Wells Fargo express agencies had sprung up by 1900. The commercial letter shown here departed Chihuahua, Mexico, in May 1893, crossed the border at El Paso, and proceeded to the capital of American finance.

"Lincoln's Elected!" In 1925, Wells Fargo asked Western artist Maynard Dixon to depict a pony rider pounding through Placerville with this electrifying news. The 1860 presidential result reached San Francisco on November 14 in a record seven days, 17 hours. After five changes of horses over 75 miles, each rider passed the letter-holding mochilla to the next, and the mail rushed forward over the 1,943-mile trail.

In 1860, William H. Russell, Alexander Majors, and William B. Waddell, partners in a Kansas freighting firm, founded the Pony Express. Pictured here, this letter to San Francisco commission merchants Charles W. Crosby and Albert Dibblee indicates that the fee stood high, at $5 a half-ounce. Despite the cost, Californians celebrated the 10-day news delivery.

Slow government payments to Russell, Majors, and Waddell and the resulting financial shenanigans sent the owners of the Pony Express into bankruptcy. To keep the fast mail service running, on April 15, 1861, Wells Fargo became "agent" for its operations west of Salt Lake City. Wells Fargo promptly had San Francisco lithographers Joseph Britton and Jacques Joseph Rey produce stamps carrying the Wells Fargo name.

No matter how hard the gallant riders rushed their fast steeds, they could not outrun electricity. On October 24, 1861, the overland telegraph joined in Salt Lake City. After 18 months running time, the Pony Express was no more. *Harper's Weekly*, on November 2, 1867, depicted its approaching demise.

In 1923, Californians resolved to break the 1860 pony-express record made delivering the news of Lincoln's election, and Wells Fargo commissioned artist Maynard Dixon to create a small gold medal to present to winning participants. Those opening savings accounts during a specified time received bronze copies. At the California line, William S. Tevis, a grandson of Wells Fargo president Lloyd Tevis, alone raced the U.S. Cavalry and won. From this feat, in 1955, the Western States Trail Foundation's "100 Miles One Day Pony Express Ride" emerged. Today the Tevis Cup rewards the winner of the world's oldest endurance race for man and horse.

Four

STAGECOACHING

The stagecoach meant public transportation. Government contracts to stagecoach companies to carry the U.S. mail subsidized road building, mandated regular scheduling, and facilitated travelers. Often when the government awarded a new mail contract, ownership of the stage line changed, too.

Stage companies picked up additional income carrying the money-laden treasure boxes of express companies, and between 1852 and 1918, Wells Fargo made such contracts. During the 1870s, for instance, Wells Fargo provided a solid five and a half percent to the gross revenues of the Coast Line Stage Company, running between San Francisco and Los Angeles.

For most of the 1850s, California steamships provided the only communication with the rest of the United States. In 1857, Congress worked to increase mail frequency and decrease delivery time. Since a land route provided the solution, Congress authorized an overland-mail route between St. Louis, Missouri, and San Francisco, California, and invited bids.

John Butterfield, vice president of the American Express Company, formed the Overland Mail Company to bid on the government mail contract, just as Federal Express and United Parcel Service do today. Express companies staked out geographical areas of the United States for monopolized business, and Butterfield invited those whose territory encompassed the route. Directors and stockholders of the American, Adams, and United States Express Companies, as well as Wells, Fargo & Company invested in the new enterprise.

In 1858, semiweekly Overland Mail Company stagecoaches rolled across the Southwest, and in 1860, joint Wells Fargo directors came to control this company. The Civil War brought a central route through Salt Lake City, and on July 1, 1861, a daily mail service. As mining booms were spreading eastward through Nevada, Idaho, and Montana, Wells Fargo opened a Salt Lake City office in 1865 to tap gold flowing into the city.

Montana and Idaho gold heading to eastern financial centers tempted Wells Fargo. This treasure went into stagecoach king Ben Holladay's Salt Lake bank and out over his routes to New York. If Wells Fargo wished to extend its sphere of influence, it had to pay the huge price Holladay set on his banking, express, and stagecoach empire. He claimed to have 110 coaches, 1,750 horses, and 450 employees.

Wells Fargo bought out Holladay and received lasting benefits. On November 1, 1866, Wells Fargo changed from a time-limited, joint-stock association to an unlimited Colorado incorporated company. With this move, Wells Fargo combined several short lines into a record 3,000 miles of stagecoaching, gained a profitable Salt Lake City bank, and secured for its service area all territory from California to the Missouri River.

Stagecoach passengers experienced a welcome change. Holladay's fares moved with the market, usually up. In contrast, Wells Fargo published fixed prices, dropped the cost per mile, and discharged employees for "incivility to passengers."

Wells Fargo lost heavily in the stagecoach business, but when the railroad came, Wells Fargo was aboard. The "iron horse" in 1869 extended Wells Fargo's reach throughout Kansas and Nebraska.

"Old Charlie," as artist J. Ross Browne depicted him, represents the proverbial stage driver for the multitude of stage companies that carried Wells Fargo's treasure boxes. Charles D. Parkhurst was one such "Old Charlie." In 1853, he drove for John Dillon and Nelson Hedge's U.S. mail line, which ran 50 miles daily between San Francisco and San Jose. At other times, he drank, swore, voted, and farmed. In 1879, those mourning his death received the shock of their lives when they discovered that Parkhurst was actually a woman!

Wells Fargo's Louis McLane is forever linked with stagecoaching. One of his companies ran from Sacramento to Portland, Oregon. In the early 1870s, Wells Fargo officer Aaron Stein sketched "Stagecoach Passing Mount Shasta." Ever the realist, McLane confessed, "Staging looked very well when lithographed, but was the devil in reality."

On March 3, 1857, Congress approved overland mail, and the postmaster general picked a 2,800-mile route from Missouri to California by way of Texas. To bid on the contract, John Butterfield, then vice president of American Express, formed the Overland Mail Company through a combination of directors from the four express companies along the route. Wells Fargo financed the line to El Paso, and Adams Express looked to the eastern leg. On September 16, 1858, the Overland Mail Company began a 25-day, semiweekly schedule.

CEREMONIES

HONORING OVERLAND MAIL CENTENNIAL COMMEMORATIVE STAMP

SAN FRANCISCO, OCTOBER 10, 1958

While waiting for a transcontinental railroad, Californians avidly adopted faster mail transportation by stage. By 1860, stagecoaches transported more letters than steamers did. "The people here are half frantic with joy," a San Franciscan wrote in October 1858. "We feel *nearer* to our old homes." Even the fussy postmaster general admitted that mail came "with great regularity, and generally within the scheduled time."

The overland mail used graceful Concord coaches at the ends of the line; for the middle, James Goold & Company, of Albany, New York, constructed rugged, canvas-topped "celerity" wagons. Allegedly swift, they were in reality cramped. Two sets of three passengers faced each other, interlocking knees. The interior of the wagon could only contain 10 of 12 legs.

On December 11, 1858, *Harper's Weekly* depicted a curious crowd of 20 people aboard an overland stage preparing to depart San Francisco's Portsmouth Plaza. This scene stands in contrast to the first arrival in the Bay City. At 1:00 a.m. on October 10, 1858, the mail stage rushed through San Jose with the driver blowing his horn, horses snorting, iron horse shoes clanging, and coach rattling. Alarmed, "there arose simultaneously throughout the city," the paper reported, "the loud, deep note of warning from the whole canine race." Later that Sunday morning, the coach noisily pulled into the quiet Portsmouth Square terminus, quickly rushing to the post office three blocks away. Finally, at 7:30 a.m., 23 days and 23.5 hours after leaving St. Louis, a sleepy postal clerk stumbled to the door to receive the first overland mail delivery.

In the spring of 1861, as the Civil War erupted throughout the nation, the route shifted north—but not before a Texas photographer shot driver David McLaughlin driving a rugged "celerity wagon." One traveler across the dry plains of Texas and the deserts of the Southwest complained of being caked with "a thick coating of alkali dust," going wild from the "prickly heat," and only partially surviving on a monotonous "diet of boiled black beans" and coffee.

In 1859, two years after stagecoaches first rolled over the Sierra, eccentric Horace Greeley, editor of the *New York Tribune*, followed advice he often dispensed, "Go West, young man!" As his westbound stage arrived at Strawberry, the last telegraph station, 50 miles from Placerville, Greeley became nervous. "Driver," he said condescendingly, "can you get me into Placerville this evening by 5 o'clock, because the Committee expects me, and I do not wish to disappoint them." With emphasis, he added, "Do not promise unless you are certain." Driver Hank Monk, participant in a prestigious profession, picked up the ribbons, and said quietly, "I'll get you there."

Hank Monk's coach speedily rushed down steep Sierra Nevada slopes with Greeley, as humorist Mark Twain enjoyed telling, bouncing around—the buttons popping off his coat. Finally, Greeley's head shot through the roof. "Driver, I'm not particular for an hour or two," the shaken passenger expostulated. "Horace, keep your seat!" Monk retorted. "I told you I would get you there by 5 o'clock, and by God, I'll do it." Readers of the *Tribune* received sound advice from the distraught scribbler, "I cannot conscientiously recommend the route I have traveled to summer tourists in quest of pleasure."

In 1860, Louis McLane, Wells Fargo's general manager, bought the Pioneer Stage Company as a private investment, and placed his brother Charles in charge. By 1864, the Pioneer Stage Company ran three stagecoaches a day in each direction, transporting 60 passengers total between San Francisco and Virginia City, Nevada. This photograph shows a fully loaded Concord coach drawn by six matched white horses as it prepares to depart Wells Fargo's office in Virginia City.

Gold rush photographer William Shew produced this table of distances for the Pioneer Stage Company about the time Wells Fargo purchased it in December 1864. Its destinations also reflect silver rushes to Alpine County and Austin, Nevada.

Pioneer Stage Route,

Via LAKE BIGLER, or TAHOE,

SACRAMENTO to VIRGINIA CITY

ESMERALDA REESE RIVER AND HUMBOLDT.

Via S. V. R. R'ds & P. & V. R. R'ds.

			Miles.	
Sacramento,	-	- -	0	
Folsom,	by Rail Road,		22	
Latrobe,	" "	"	15	37
Placerville,	by Stage,		16	
Sportman's Hall,	"	"	11	
River-Side Station,	"	"	10	
Webster's,	"	"	9½	
Strawberry Valley,	"	"	11	
Yank's,	"	"	11	
Lake Bigler,	"	"	9	
Glenbrook,	"	"	9	
Carson,	"	"	13½	
Virginia City,	"	"	16	116
Geneva to Markleeville,		"	25	
" " Esmeralda,		"	94	
Carson to Reese River,		"	170	
" " Star City,		"	165	

WILLIAM SHEW,
PHOTOGRAPHER,
No. 423 Montgomery Street,
SAN FRANCISCO.

"Oh, Nell, I wish you could see the scenery of these mountains," one stage rider exclaimed to his eastern sister, "For once everything you ever saw would look tame when compared with it." What a ride it was. "My seat is on the box with the Driver, as it always is when I can get it. Now we are off on a run. Up hill and down makes no difference." In the mid-1860s, artists William Keith and Charles and Hugo Nahl depicted a Wells Fargo stagecoach arriving at a Sierra station—perhaps Zephyr Cove, bordering the eastern shore of the clear shimmering waters of Lake Tahoe.

At Strawberry station, a heavily loaded Nevada-bound coach pauses for the camera. A spare coach at left shows the arrangement of topside seating cushions. Drivers changed here, halfway between Placerville and Carson. The old driver waited to take his coach west 41 miles, back to Placerville. The new reinsman and his stage continued 43 miles east to Carson City. Drivers changed their six horses every 10 miles.

DANGEROUS BOULDERS.

Interior coach accommodations came cramped. "Feet are dovetailed under seats; elbows are drawn nearer; and crinoline doubled," said one woman of a typical trip. Another passenger wedged himself between two ladies. Starting out, he did not have "six inches of seat," but the jouncing and bouncing of the coach quickly "settled me down," he wrote.

Freight wagons stand in the foreground as a pioneer stagecoach approaches the Slippery Ford House. The Sierra Bluffs exemplified the spectacular scenery along the way and are a favorite today. Closer to view, one woman remarked that "the whole route is lined with empty bottles." Why not? One journalist moralized, "If you have anything to take in a bottle, pass it around. A man who drinks by himself in such a case is lost to all human feeling."

Today, from U.S. Highway 50, the site of the Slippery Ford House lies in the cleft between the two peaks. The pioneering automobile Lincoln Highway went this way also. Now bypassed, trees have grown over the area, while rock climbers enjoy climbing the sheer bluffs.

On July 7, 1865, Speaker of the House Schuyler Colfax arrived at Yank's Station, the easternmost stop in California, and posed for the camera before setting out. That evening, in Placerville, Colfax declared, "It requires more nerve, talent and genius to be a stage driver in these mountains for Wells, Fargo & Company than it does [to be] an ordinary congressman like myself."

Continuous commerce to the Comstock divided use of the well-graded road. Freight wagons had it during the day, and Pioneer Stage Coaches had it at night. At Strawberry, in late July 1863, a traveler, with permission, climbed up on the box with the driver. "We are now on the highest point," he said. "I have to put a new candle in the lamp and off we start. Lake Bigler [Tahoe] still and shining hundreds of feet below. We go down such turns. I had perfect confidence in this driver. He said we must make time down the mountain, so I *let him go* and we did."

As Wells Fargo expanded eastward in the 1860s, it encountered Benjamin Holladay (1819–1887). In 1862, Holladay bought the failing Central Overland California and Pike's Peak Express Company, a Kansas incorporated company. If Wells Fargo wished to ride the railroad to the Missouri River, Holladay said, "They must pay our toll for crossing our bridge." On November 1, 1866, President Louis McLane paid Holladay's toll.

The Abbot-Downing Company of Concord, New Hampshire, built many wagons but only one coach. The rigors of the road demanded extra sturdy nine-passenger vehicles, and Wells Fargo ordered those with the candle lamps "extra large" and all iron and leather materials "extra stout." Vermillion bodies, light yellow undercarriages, and landscape scenes on the doors completed the look of Wells Fargo's 2,200-pound beauties.

William H. "Shotgun" Taylor, dressed here for a Montana winter, exemplified Wells Fargo's superintendents. His nickname came from an incident where he pulled a short-barreled shotgun on a bully. Once stage driver Taylor raced from Strawberry to Placerville in three and a half hours, "the fastest time at 50 miles ever made with a six horse coach in California," he bragged. In Montana, Superintendent Taylor continually cut time and improved accomodations.

In 1867, Wells Fargo added 40 new coaches, nearly one-third of its fleet: first, an order of 10, and then one of 30. On April 15, 1868, a railroad pulled out of Concord, New Hampshire, carrying 30 stagecoaches, the largest order Abbot-Downing ever filled. Bound for Wells Fargo, the train went straight through to Omaha, Nebraska. There Wells Fargo parceled them out as needed. A large contingent went to Montana. One of them, No. 251, is in Wells Fargo's Old Town San Diego History Museum. In 1928, Wells Fargo Bank repurchased one from the first order. Since then, No. 186 has greeted visitors to Wells Fargo's San Francisco museum. The Concord stagecoach became a symbol of Wells Fargo's universal service.

On April 1, 1867, after a horrible winter, Wells Fargo got its transcontinental stagecoach empire moving and published fares comparable to those for airline flights today. Wells Fargo's through tickets cost 17¢ per mile. In 1865 and 1866, market-gouging Ben Holladay charged 28 to 40¢ a mile. Elsewhere in this advertisement, Wells Fargo promised "first class conveyances, careful and experienced drivers, and attentive agents," but best of all, it banished boredom. Wells Fargo coaches rolled through "the beautiful scenery of the Rocky Mountains and the Great Plains."

GREAT OVERLAND MAIL ROUTE.

PACIFIC AND ATLANTIC STATES.

WELLS, FARGO & CO.

SOLE PROPRIETORS.

FARE REDUCED !   TIME SHORTENED !

On and after the 1st day of April, 1867, passengers will be forwarded through at the following reduced rates, viz:

Sacramento to Omaha	$300.
Virginia City to Omaha	275.
Austin to Omaha	225.
Sacramento to Cheyenne	250.
Virginia City to Cheyenne	225.
Austin to Denver	175.
Salt Lake to Bannock, Montana	120.
" Virginia	120.
" Helena	145.
" Fort Benton	175.

ALL LEGAL TENDERS OR THEIR EQUIVALENT.

12

An African American driver and his matched team prepare to pull out an ornate, fully-loaded coach from Wells Fargo's Salt Lake City banking, express, and stagecoach office. While the main line went east to Nebraska and west to California, Wells Fargo coaches also headed 400 miles to Boise, Idaho, and 700 miles to Fort Benton, Montana. (Courtesy of the Historical Department, Church of Jesus Christ of Latter-day Saints, Salt Lake City, Utah.)

For those used to graded and paved roads, the overland route was neither. Through Nevada, for instance, 13 mountain ranges ran north to south, and the east-west pony express and overland mail trail traversed them all. This view from a slate quarry at the west end of Egan Canyon looks over the former station site and across a 15-mile valley to Butte Station in the similarly designated mountains. At one end of the wooden station, a cooking stove stood to prepare endless combinations of flour, bacon, dust, and flies. The agent and hostler slept in bunks at the other end. A Goshute Indian kept the harness supply in repair, hunted, and generally helped out around the compound.

From the east, the stage road enters Egan Canyon and cuts through the Cherry Mountains. Dust-raising intrusions in the 1860s aroused local Goshutes, making stations isolated in the Nevada vastness vulnerable. Yet "courtesy," Henry Wells' one word for all relationships, worked miracles. When Don Carlos Salisbury kept station in 1867, Wells Fargo mandated that he keep peace with Native Americans. Salisbury generously loaned stewing kettles and rolled out flour barrels. "You treat them [too good]," the hotheaded hostler howled. "Treat 'em rough, I says." Salisbury retorted, "If you had been agent here, this station would have been burned weeks ago, and your bones would have been well bleached in the desert sun by now!" Courtesy prevailed; coaches kept running.

Schellbourne stood as the next station east of Egan Canyon, nestled in a stream-fed glade in the Schell Mountains, which provided year-round forage. In 1864, the Overland Mail Company built handsome whitewashed stone repair shops here. Twenty coachbuilders, wheelwrights, carpenters, and painters kept rolling stock running. Eastward, Antelope Pass rose to 7,980 feet, the highest point on the Pony Express route; overland stagecoaches preferred a longer but lower trail.

Stagecoach travel had its hazards, as this photograph taken in 1889 in Mexico indicates. Here a tourist experienced "a break-down," as he, his wife, charming daughters, and a padre journeyed south from Puebla into the mountains. The Concord coach certainly looks forlorn, but the six mules act unconcerned. (Courtesy of Bob Jernigan.)

Road builders laid logs crosswise to make corduroy roads that traversed swamps. Its uneven surface has spooked the horses in artist Charles Russell's gouache drawing hanging in the Wells Fargo History Museum in San Francisco.

Riding a coach subjected passengers to unbearable conditions, although artist Charles M. Russell portrayed a time when spooked stage horses had too much bear. Travelers expected dust without end, but could not prepare for the aerial attack. Western mosquitoes, said to be six times as large and belligerent as eastern ones, could, one traveler complained, "penetrate anything but a regular ironclad." (Original gouache drawing courtesy of the San Francisco Wells Fargo History Museum).

Rugged Wells Fargo mud wagons traversed the roughest roads, as proved in this photograph by the mud-caked wheels standing in the well-churned earth at Fort Bridger, Wyoming. Animals gravitated to station keepers, and cats, such as this one playing by the front wheel, were favorites.

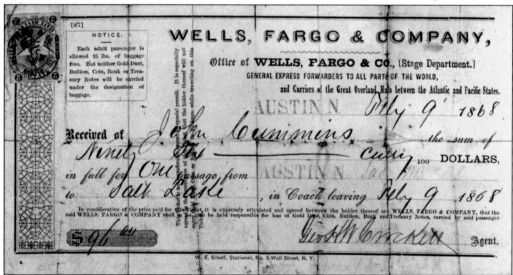

W.ᵐ A. Carter	To Wells Fargo & Co: Dr		
1868		**$**	**¢**
July 18	½ J Miller's Stage Fare Ft Bridger to Weber	13	00
" 19	1 Keg &½ 1 Box addressed to J.G. Flero Quaking Asp	12	50
" 21	Sam Dean Stage Fare from Bridger to Bear River	5	00
" 22	M.ʳˢ Lane & Servant Fare Daniels to Bridger	22	50
"	Chaˢ Sherwood Exp Box ✓	22	55
" 28	Geo Sanford Exp Box ✓	25	00
" 30	1 Pkg of Currency Exp to Omaha	5	50
" 31	1 Pkg		75
" "	1 Exp Box addressed to M.ʳˢ M.E. Carter	2	25
" "	1 Pkg of Currency Expressed from Green River	2	50

Hospitable William A. Carter, the Fort Bridger post trader, often used Wells Fargo to send money; carry friends and employees; and ship merchandise to or from Salt Lake City or Omaha. Fifty Wells Fargo franked envelopes assured Carter of quick dispatch of his orders to California merchants, while Wells Fargo agent Charles E. Catlin delivered choice eastern items to Mary E. Carter.

In February 1868, John Cummins boarded a Wells Fargo stagecoach at Austin, Nevada, bound for Salt Lake City, 390 miles and three days away. Wells Fargo protected its primary express business by forbidding Cummins to "carry Gold dust, Coin or Bullion in Package, while traveling on this Ticket." This referred to bulk shipments, not personal funds. In return, if the stage were robbed, Wells Fargo paid losses immediately. Unlike airlines, Wells Fargo measured carry-ons by weight and not by size. Twenty-five pounds did not go far.

During the 15-day overland trip, Wells Fargo coaches stopped at swing stations every 12 miles to change horses. Home stations, 45 miles apart, provided meals and sleeping accommodations. Coaches rolled along 24 hours, day after day, making 125 miles daily. Teams of horses, therefore, averaged a two-and-a-half-hour workout, while passengers could expect a meal within nine hours. Stations were not much to look at, and usually were one-story log or sod structures.

Famed French artists Paul Frenzeny and Jules Tavernier crossed the country in 1874, sketching for *Harper's Weekly*; this artwork was published on Independence Day. A few years earlier, a traveler recorded his experience in words. On January 7, 1868, with the temperature at minus 40 degrees, the Wells Fargo stage sleigh stopped at Pleasant Valley, a hundred miles south of Virginia City, Montana. Inside, tired but warm passengers enjoyed an excellent supper and then bathed sore feet. Their station keeper had an amazing story to tell. She was a Southern woman who had lost her husband and home during the war and came west to find opportunity. Wells Fargo paid her $125 to provide this cozy refuge.

Overland driver Hank Conner had the same spunk and spirit as fancily dressed James E. Johnston, shown here in 1860. In January 1868, Connor headed east from Fort Bridger, determined to give journalist Alexander K. McClure a sleigh ride to remember, as McClure told it, while the passengers resolved to "die rather than 'squeal'." A wild yell of "Git!" followed by the reverberating crack of the whip sent six wild broncos charging at a dozen miles an hour over a mountain road in the dead of night. Only passengers swinging out, as if on a sail boat, kept the sleigh from tipping, while bare spots on the road sparked a trail of fire from the iron runners. At 1:00 a.m., they pulled up to a station, and Connor was most apologetic for his slow speed.

On February 8, 1858, *Harper's Weekly* depicted a hard-pressed Wells Fargo stagecoach traversing Guy's Gulch in the Rocky Mountains during a blizzard. Wells Fargo still pushed on. "Wells, Fargo & Co. mean to do all they have contracted to do," head office decreed, "and to carry the mails without delay or damage." Of anyone in the world, the postmaster general declared, only "the American people would ever undertake to carry a mail 2,000 miles through a wilderness in a coach."

In 1892, Wells Fargo brought a Concord coach to the Chicago World's Fair to emphasize its historical exhibit and to transport dignitaries. From this beginning, its parade-coach program went nationwide. In May 1912, the coach "Charlie McLane" traversed New York City's famed Broadway, and then, appropriately, returned to the Windy City. Shown here, four dark iron grays pull at least 20 celebrating Wells Fargo employees across Lincoln Park, Chicago. Wells Fargo displays two of the three parade coaches, one in San Francisco, the other in Phoenix, Arizona.

In the mid-1950s, Wells Fargo Bank settled on the Concord coach as its logo, and in 1958, revived the stagecoach-appearance program. Beginning with a branch opening in Hayward, Sport Fellingham, and then his wife, Virginia, took the reins. Described by all who knew her as "a petite woman with a shoot-from-the-hip personality," Virginia Fellingham drove for a legendary 30 years.

Currently, Wells Fargo can put 16 stagecoaches on the road on any given day, and in 2005, 24 million people at 789 events saw Wells Fargo's "living logo."

Five

THE EXPRESS BUSINESS GROWS WITH THE NATION

Success in the express business came to those who dared. Wells Fargo placed agents and offices at places more or less remote from each other and connected them by river, rail, and road.

During the era of the railroads, that half-century between 1870 and 1920, Wells Fargo expanded throughout the nation. In 1888, it became the first express to offer an "ocean to ocean" service. Once east of the Mississippi River, Wells Fargo multiplied offices in the manufacturing areas of the Midwest and Northeast.

Railroads and express companies had joint interests in express contracts. The express business stood as the most valuable portion of railroad freight, but it was time consuming and complex. Some railroads formed their own express companies, but an easier way of control came through stock ownership in independent express companies. The Southern Pacific and Santa Fe Railroads placed directors on Wells Fargo's board.

In the early 1880s, rail lines reached everywhere, and ice-cooled refrigerated cars became common. In 1898, Wells Fargo ordered its first such "reefers," and within 15 years, it had 150. These were special cars, equipped to be coupled with high-speed passenger trains. With them, Wells Fargo developed markets for carloads of agricultural produce.

Yet horsepower served the more remote places of the West, even into the 1920s. Money traveling in stagecoaches on isolated roads proved tempting to highwaymen, and Wells Fargo sent armed guards, the famed "shotgun messengers," with valuable shipments. In the 1880s, though, daring outlaws specialized in more lucrative railroad robbery. The agent nearest a holdup contacted the county sheriff and coordinated pursuit. As backup, Wells Fargo formed a determined detective force, never numbering more than a half-dozen, to capture the bad men.

Wells Fargo's two late-19th-century presidents ably guided the company. In 1869, corporate raider Lloyd Tevis (1824–1899) engineered the Central Pacific/Southern Pacific Railroad takeover of Wells Fargo and became president. For one-third of its stock, Wells Fargo received an exclusive express contract on the railroad, enabling it to expand. During his 20 years, from 1872 to 1892, Tevis invigorated Wells Fargo's banking and, through notable negotiation, extended the express service across the continent.

In 1892, John J. Valentine (1840–1901) followed Tevis. Since the late 1860s, he had supervised the express business with a humanist philosophy. "The rights of man are of more importance than the paltry consideration of the dollar," President Valentine declared in 1900. For the world, he led Wells Fargo to organize relief efforts for sufferers from fire, flood, and pestilence. For employees, he personally bought circulating libraries to encourage self-improvement. Speaking for Wells Fargo, Valentine stated simply, "In the administration of our affairs, we appeal to all that is fairest and open and best."

Tevis and Valentine paid particular attention to financial services. "The business is one requiring prompt care and attention to all its details," Wells Fargo mandated, and money matters were most important. For those in a hurry, beginning in 1864, Wells Fargo transferred money electronically through the telegraph. In that same year, the U.S. Post Office instituted a cumbersome mail process to pay money throughout the United States.

In 1882, the American Express Company adapted a simpler money-order system, suitable for express companies. Valentine believed such money transfers fostered "intimacy" between Wells Fargo and its customers, and in December 1885, Wells Fargo offered money orders through 1,600 agencies. From such simple cash transfers, mail-order houses, such as Montgomery Ward and Sears, Roebuck & Company flourished. The latter's 1897 catalogue stated, "We recommend the express money order system because it is inexpensive, of less trouble, and is safe; besides this, if it should get lost or miscarried your loss will be made good." Due to all of these conveniences, some bankers felt selling express money orders would be cheaper for banks than cashing checks for $50 or less. Wells Fargo traveler's checks, an 1891 American Express innovation, arrived in 1903.

In the early 20th century, numerous express companies blanketed the nation, but only one captured and kept the romance of the business: Wells Fargo. Wells Fargo worked hard to maintain that image. In 1918, it operated 10,000 offices over 120,000 miles of railroad, steamship, and stagecoach lines. It had offices in Alaska and Hawaii; Cuba, El Salvador, Mexico, and Panama; and China and the Philippines. Connections sent Wells Fargo's express worldwide.

As Eastern European immigrants pressed into the United States, Wells Fargo saw to their needs. In 1913, it introduced foreign-language postal remittances tailored for Italians, Hungarians, Slavs, Poles, Russians, and Scandinavians. They facilitated sending money home to isolated, bankless villages that were reached only by a national letter service. Currently Wells Fargo has a similar electronic system for Mexico, the Philippines, India, and China.

During World War I, the federal government seized the nation's railroads to coordinate shipments of war materials. A logical extension led to the combination of the domestic express business on July 1, 1918. Into American Railway Express went Adams Express; American Express; the U.S. operations of the Canadian Express; Great Northern Express; National Express; Southern Express; Wells Fargo & Company Express; and Western Express.

Not much of Wells Fargo & Company Express remained. The company had its traveler's checks and money orders, an inoperative Mexican subsidiary and an operating Cuban one. In 1919, American Express Company purchased these Wells Fargo businesses to combine Wells Fargo's financial paper with its own. It, too, had lost its express delivery business in 1918, and American Express survived by expanding its tourist business and related financial services. It still dominates the traveler's-check market.

With American Express Company owning a majority of its stock, Wells Fargo & Company president Elmer R. Jones kept Cuba and expanded business in Mexico. In addition to expressing, Wells Fargo become Mexico's largest travel company, sold American agricultural machinery there, and imported Mexican agricultural produce into the United States. Wells Fargo's U.S. expressing service revived in 1938, when it purchased an armored car business. When Wells Fargo & Company became inoperative in the mid-1960s, American Express Company sold Wells Fargo Armored Car Service to Baker Industries. In 1997, it became part of Loomis, Fargo & Company.

In this spring 1867 photograph, rail meets road. The Central Pacific Railroad stopped at Cisco, while Chinese workers blasted and chipped tunnels through the Sierra summit. Wells Fargo agent Nelson Hammond, between the train and left coach, prepares to dispatch three heavily loaded Wells Fargo stagecoaches on to Virginia City. Hammond followed the progress of the railroad, as he successively became Wells Fargo agent at Dutch Flat in 1865; Alta in 1866; Cisco in 1867; and Reno in 1868.

John J. Valentine left his birth state of Kentucky in 1862 for California, where he joined Wells Fargo as agent at Strawberry. As a man of strong opinions, a newspaper noted, "He seems to thrive on labor and perplexities." Within six years, Valentine ran Wells Fargo's expressing operations and continued to do so until he became president in 1892. Above all, Valentine was a humanist, and at his 1901 funeral, his company mourned him as "Our Guide and Friend."

Wells Fargo president Lloyd Tevis abruptly greeted visitors: "Talk quickly, and to the point—I can think five times as fast as any man in San Francisco." This statement would have been arrogance in a lesser man, but all agreed Tevis excelled at negotiation. Business ventures included the California Steam Navigation Company, California State Telegraph Company, San Francisco Gas Company, Pacific Ice Company, Spring Valley Water Company, and the Risdon Iron Works. With his brother-in-law, James Ben Ali Haggin, Tevis owned huge swaths of California agricultural land, as well as the Homestake gold mining company of South Dakota, and the Anaconda copper mine of Butte, Montana.

Wells Fargo's railroad-express business often blended express, railroad, and telegraph agents together. One combination person wrote, "I am alone; have all the operating to do and all way-billing. It makes a fellow hustle to keep up and not get trains muddled up." Another such talented three-part individual was Cassie Tomer Hill, agent at Roseville from 1884 to 1908. This widowed mother raised five children, ran a business, and lived to be 100 years old.

The receipt seen here reverse sums up Wells Fargo's services, from delivery to finance. Historian Carl Wheat remarked that Wells Fargo "went everywhere, did almost anything for anybody, and was the nearest thing to a universal service company ever invented."

On January 1, 1867, the PMSS *Colorado* inaugurated direct mail and Wells Fargo express service with Japan and China, stopping at Yokohama and Hong Kong. The wooden 360-foot sidewheel paddler *China*, pictured docked in San Francisco, joined the *Colorado* in October to cross 5,200 miles of ocean. Broken up in the early 1880s, the *China's* ornate deck cabin survives in Belvedere, Marin County.

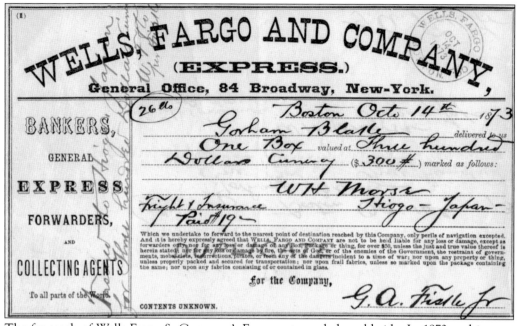

WELLS, FARGO AND COMPANY,
(EXPRESS.)
General Office, 84 Broadway, New-York.

BANKERS,

GENERAL

EXPRESS

FORWARDERS,

AND

COLLECTING AGENTS

To all parts of the World.

26 *Uo*

Boston Octo 14th 1873

Gorham Blake delivered to us

One Box valued at *Three hundred Dollars Currency* ($ *300* #) marked as follows:

WH Morse

Freight & Insurance *Hiogo — Japan —*

Paid $19 —

Which we undertake to forward to the nearest point of destination reached by this Company, only perils of navigation excepted. And it is hereby expressly agreed that WELLS, FARGO AND COMPANY are not to be held liable for any loss or damage, except as forwarders only, nor for any loss or damage of any Box, package or thing, for over $50, unless the just and true value thereof is herein stated; nor for any loss or damage by fire, the acts of God, or of the enemies of the Government, the restraint of governments, mobs, riots, insurrections, pirates, or from any of the dangers incident to a time of war; nor upon any property or thing, unless properly packed and secured for transportation; nor upon frail fabrics, unless so marked upon the package containing the same; nor upon any fabrics consisting of or contained in glass.

For the Company,

G. A. Fiske jr

CONTENTS UNKNOWN.

The far reach of Wells Fargo & Company's Express expanded worldwide. In 1873, a shipment of silverware left Boston to travel across the continent on the transcontinental railroad. On November 1, 1873, the *Colorado* carried it over the Pacific to Yokohama. The Pacific Mail Steamship Company also served several Japanese ports and Shanghai, and its dependable gold rush steamer *Golden Age* carried the silver plate to the trade treaty port of Hiogo (Kobe), Japan. It arrived on December 3, 1873, about seven weeks after departing Boston.

As a glistening railroad chuffs away from Napa in 1892, engineer, crew, and Wells Fargo's messenger smile for the camera, while a colorfully painted Wells Fargo delivery wagon stuffed with packages prepares to make its delivery rounds.

Entrepreneurial sisters Lucy Miller and Julia Jones kept the Wells Fargo office at Mariposa between 1885 and 1909. Not only did Miller, recently widowed with a young son, run the Wells Fargo office, but she became postmaster as well. These combined duties saw her up at 5:00 a.m. to send off the stagecoach to Merced. In 1892, Julia Jones replaced her sister. Although Jones was deemed legally not competent to vote due to gender, male voters elected her for three terms as county superintendent of schools. In 1902, she returned the office to her sister, who ran it until she remarried in 1909. For 24 years, two able women served Wells Fargo. In 1911, California became the sixth state to grant women the right to vote.

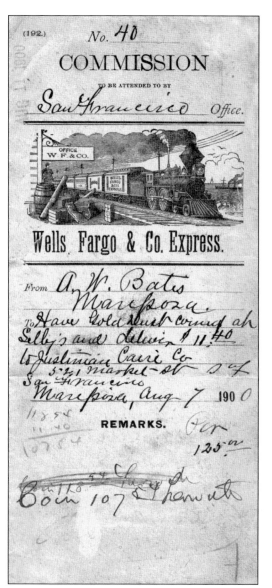

Pictured here, a Wells Fargo commission envelope in 1900 contained a request for two services. Armand W. Bates asked Mariposa agent Julia Jones to send gold dust to the Selby refinery in Contra Costa County. From the returns, he asked, would Wells Fargo's San Francisco office please pay $11.40 to the Justinian Caire Company, dealers in assayers' materials, and return the rest to him? Of course, and $107.54 in coin came to Bates. Commissions were one of Wells Fargo's special services, performed for customers at a distance from each other.

North and south of the Mexican border, Wells Fargo delivered currency safely in money envelopes. Regulations declared that envelopes and the money inside be stitched through, with the twine ends sealed with brittle wax to prevent and reveal tampering.

Beginning with Guaymas in 1860, Wells Fargo served West Coast Mexican ports, and after Mexican president Porfirio Diaz expanded the railroads, Supt. John J. Valentine saw opportunity. In January 1882, he wished to know "who of our employees, agents, clerks, messengers, drivers, porters, etc., speak and write the SPANISH LANGUAGE." A year later, Wells Fargo had 42 Mexican offices. In 1886, the Wells Fargo guidebook-catalogue, such as the one pictured here, informed Mexican customers about the great bounty of available American-produced merchandise—all of which would come via Wells Fargo.

In 1855, Wells Fargo opened an office in Los Angeles and advertised through the *Los Angeles Star*. These early seeds rooted. In 1872, *La Cronica* regularly listed out-of-town customers with packages waiting at the Los Angeles Wells Fargo office. Among them were Californio Maria Dominguez, a 56-year-old farmer's wife who owned $3,000 worth of property; Mexican-American farmer Jose Maria Fuentes, 55, who had a 31-year-old wife and six children under 12; and Californio Eduardo Pollorena of Los Nietos, who ran the family estate. Pollorena owned $31,000 worth of real estate and had $10,000 in personal property.

Pictured here in San Francisco about 1888, a dapper Wells Fargo wagon driver pauses in front of two Battery Street cigar merchants. Two matched white horses draw his burnished blue-sided, red-wheeled wagon. Gold lettering makes the "Wells Fargo" name pop out, while the bulldog on a strongbox symbolizes security.

In the early 1870s, the English-born Civil War veteran Charles Wells Banks proved to Wells Fargo that he was "a first-class accountant," and in 1884, became the cashier for the express department. The well-liked, genial Banks spent freely, hobnobbed at the prestigious Union and Bohemian Clubs, knew French cooking and wine, and scientifically studied things under a microscope. Yet, on November 1, 1886, hidden from Wells Fargo, he departed for Rarotonga in the Cook Islands, near New Zealand. Wells Fargo, unknowingly, had "donated" $40,000 to support a high life and a girlfriend or two! In 1892, a Wells Fargo auditor visited Banks and began a correspondence—but Banks never left the island.

WELLS, FARGO & CO'S EXPRESS.
$1,000 REWARD!

CHARLES WELLS BANKS, who up to November 1, 1886.

From the earliest days of the express business, dogs were "alert and faithful" companions, who symbolized security. In the late 1880s, Wells Fargo considered formally adopting "Jack" as a logo. When Californians celebrated the "Days of Gold, the Days of Old, the Days of '49" at San Francisco's 1894 midwinter fair, Wells Fargo representative Lew I. Bay sold souvenir photographs of his tough little bulldog puppy "Jack" on a treasure box. "Touch it if you Dare!" Jack woofed.

徐成章

The demeanor of merchant Chu Sing Jung in this 1864 photograph indicates that he stood no foolishness. Of course, he used Wells Fargo to send and receive money, mail, and merchandise because Wells Fargo built trust. In 1860, the agent in Columbia delivered $10 to the wrong Chinese man, and the owner complained to San Francisco that "he could gain no satisfaction." Headquarters responded, telling the agent, "You should be very careful," and ordered him to "Pay the proper party $10."

On Kee was in tune with Wells Fargo. In 1861, for one-half percent of its value, he safely sent $230 from Drytown, Amador County, to Chung Mow in Sacramento.

Though the 1870s and early 1880s, Wells Fargo regularly issued bilingual directories of Chinese business houses, such as the one pictured here. Openly opposing anti-Chinese sentiment, Wells Fargo steadfastly befriended the Chinese. It advertised in 1888, "The officers and employees of Wells, Fargo & Co. believe that increase in business is secured by superior service and promptitude, together with fair dealing and courtesy to all."

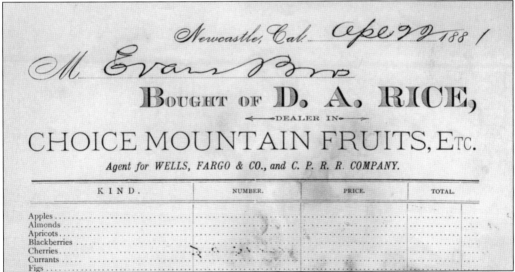

For 30 years, Rice family members ran Wells Fargo's Newcastle office. Placer County's location along the cross-country railroad, coupled with its fine soil and fair climate, led it to excel in fruit-raising. Express and railroad agent Rice presented a page of choice fruits he would dispatch to eastern markets.

In 1895, 25-year-old Ella Myers (center below) opened the Wells Fargo office in the Texas Trunk Railroad depot in Crandall, Texas, southeast of Dallas. Using crutches and being a woman were no impediments for Myers, an inquiring reporter discovered in 1899. Impressed by her abilities as a railroad-express-telegraph agent, he strongly denounced the "foolish social conservatism" that would keep women in "a condition of barbarism." Wells Fargo's route agent found Myers' work "always done in a neat, orderly manner."

In July 1880, a junk collector stole 11 large cans of tallow from an Antioch butcher shop and escaped aboard his 27-foot sloop. On July 9, town constable Dennis M. Pitts wrote on Wells Fargo stationery to San Francisco police chief Patrick Crowley. He warned that the sloop *Red Wood City* "goes into the City at Dewey's Wharf to day," and "if you find any tallow in cans on board of the sloop, arrest and telegraph me." Constable Pitts quickly sent his note on the railroad—by Wells Fargo, of course. A scrawled "Arrested by [Officer Theodore C.] Metzler" told the outcome.

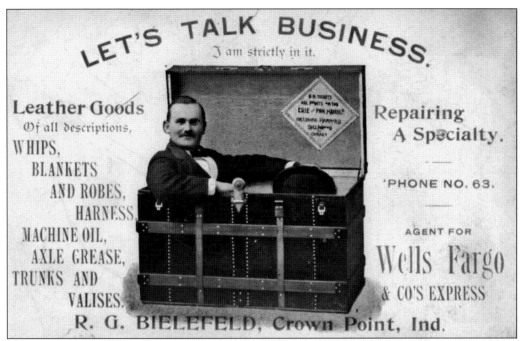

LET'S TALK BUSINESS.

I am strictly in it.

Leather Goods
Of all descriptions,
WHIPS,
BLANKETS
AND ROBES,
HARNESS,
MACHINE OIL,
AXLE GREASE,
TRUNKS AND
VALISES.

Repairing
A Specialty.

'PHONE NO. 63.

AGENT FOR

Wells Fargo
& CO'S EXPRESS

R. G. BIELEFELD, Crown Point, Ind.

Agent R. G. Bielefeld, a 20-year veteran in Crown Point, Indiana, certainly had faith in his trunks. No wonder Bielefeld could advertise, "I am strictly in it." Not only did he sell leather goods of all descriptions, but Bielefeld sold railroad tickets on the Chicago and Erie Railroad and for all points on the Erie system. Then, as now, Wells Fargo extended an invitation to customers, "Let's Talk Business."

An 1897 Arizona territory guide declared, "The resident agents of Wells, Fargo & Co. are always the repositories of valuable information respecting the conditions of business at their stations." In this 1880 photograph, Wells Fargo agent George E. Loring stands in front of his bazaar in downtown Phoenix. Additionally, watchmaker Loring sold newspapers, cigars, jewelry, dry goods, and groceries, and Native American art from this adobe on Washington Street near Center Street.

In the distance from Highway 50, "The Loneliest Road in America," Treasure Hill looms, over 9,000 feet high. In 1868, Treasure City mushroomed on the far side of this remote peak. Its rich silver deposits, ordinarily averaging 10 pounds per ton—but as free silver, reaching up to 1,400 pounds per ton—were close to the surface. Naturally, Treasure City had a Wells Fargo office, and banking genius Homer S. King ran it. By 1870, boom times had moved elsewhere, although the post office remained until 1880.

Stage driver James Wales Miller proudly exemplified Nevada's silver age, with silver stars on his hat, a silver-banded whip, and a huge silver watch and chain. During the rush to the White Pine Silver Mining District at the close of the 1860s, Wells Fargo ran a stage line into the new bonanza. One day, Miller outran would-be stagecoach robbers. What did he wish from Wells Fargo for saving the treasure? "A damn big bullion watch!" he replied. The approximately three-by-one-inch watch weighed almost one and a half pounds; the long chain added another pound. Miller wears it here.

In this 1912 photograph, schoolteacher Ann O'Brien visits Wells Fargo in Hamilton, once the White Pine County seat.

Into the 1950s, the front of this six-arched building stood two stories tall. All that remains today of the Wells Fargo building is one lone arch. Scant mortar binding light, locally made, reddish brick is not up to freezing in cold winters and roasting during hot summers. Through the remaining arch, Treasure Hill, three miles in the distance, rises another 1,000 feet.

Pictured here about 1888, a confident Wells Fargo city deliveryman faces the camera, hat brim shiny and chest badge burnished. Wells Fargo insisted on exact records, allowing this Wells Fargo wagon driver to proudly display his delivery book.

In 1876, the satirical *San Francisco Wasp* stung readers with this illustration about "traveling under difficulties on the Pacific Coast," as three masked highwaymen prepare to go through the passengers. "First come, best served" determined stagecoach seating, and a Chinese man with a sun-protecting umbrella claimed the seat of honor next to the driver.

From 1862 to 1906, Joseph Y. Ayer and his son Joseph S. Ayer made Wells Fargo's famed treasure boxes and packing trunks at their carpentry shop at 3470 Seventeenth Street in San Francisco. In the 1890s, Grandpa Ayer stands proudly to the right, while his precious granddaughter sits on two of the large Wells Fargo railroad trunks, used to protect smaller packages in shipment. Meanwhile, four carpenters eye 15 treasure boxes, some sadly in need of great repair.

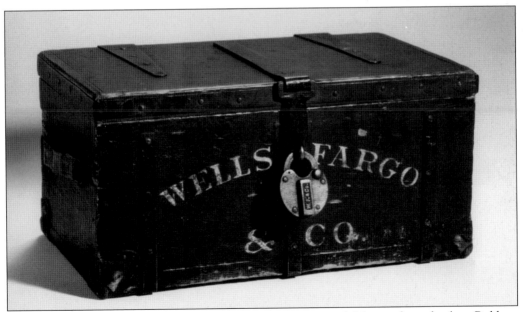

Irresistible temptation came in the form of a green, iron-strapped, 24-pound wooden box. Robbers were not so much interested in obtaining J. Y. Ayer's stout 20-by-12-by-10-inch creations as they were in the gold contained within them. These earned the name "treasure box," and aboard stagecoaches, they rested beneath the driver's feet.

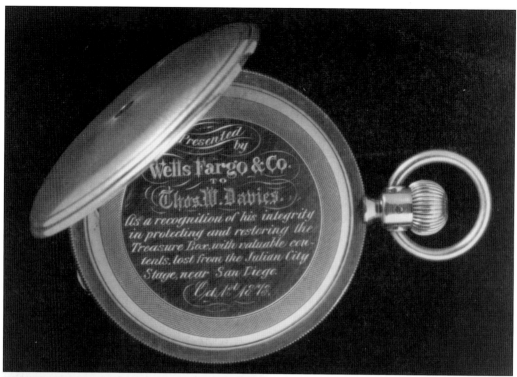

On October 1, 1873, a stagecoach driver left Julian, California, carrying $10,000 worth of gold from the Golden Chariot Mine. As the coach tipped too far forward, the driver placed the 60 pounds of boxed bullion in back, but the treasure box did not arrive in San Diego. The next morning, Thomas W. Davies, who grew olives at the old mission, returned his roadside find to Wells Fargo. Quickly, and "in recognition of his integrity," Supt. John J. Valentine sent Davies a splendid gold watch that visitors to Wells Fargo's Old Town San Diego History Museum may view.

Mike Tovey, a six-and-a-half-foot embodiment of responsibility, lived dangerously. In 1872, he became a Wells Fargo guard, armed with a short-barreled shotgun. The most dangerous routes were his. Twenty years later, Tovey still rode shotgun—until June 15, 1893. "He was shot and instantly killed by a robber who attempted to hold up the stage in which he was traveling as guard," his monument in Jackson, California, reads. "Erected as a tribute of respect by his employer, Wells, Fargo & Co."

Stagecoach robber Milton A. Sharp was persistent. In 1880, working with W. C. Jones, he robbed the Carson City to Bodie stage on June 8 and 15, and again on September 4 and 5. The incoming stagecoach carried minted gold coin; the outbound one had huge, heavy bullion bars. On this final robbery, Wells Fargo shotgun messenger Mike Tovey killed Jones, but Sharp, in turn, wounded Tovey. While Tovey went to have his wound treated, Sharp returned and robbed the stage. Wells Fargo detective Jim Hume shortly tracked him down and sent him to prison.

M. A. Sharp

Robbed Bodie Stage four times in June & Sept. 1880 with Frank Dorr.

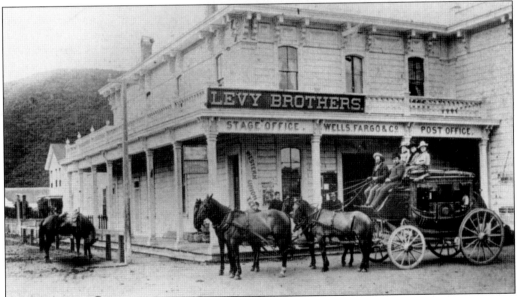

On August 17, 1905, a black-masked desperado, described as "nine feet high" and "armed with a small cannon," stopped the Half Moon Bay stagecoach. He angrily ordered driver Ed Campbell to throw down Wells, Fargo & Company's treasure box, Levy Brothers strongbox, and the U.S. mailbag. There were no valuables among them, and the five passengers hid their gold. The robber gained only $4.30, and so ended stagecoach robbery in San Mateo County.

After a strenuous El Dorado County peace officer apprenticeship, James B. Hume became Wells Fargo's chief detective from 1873 until his death in 1904. He was the model investigator, methodically collecting evidence, rigidly analyzing cases, minutely compiling data, shrewdly judging character, and never giving up. His 1885 *Robbers' Record* listed and described outlaws to aid sheriffs throughout the West.

In early August 1879, acting Arizona governor John J. Gosper proclaimed a reward of $500 for each dead highwayman. His words elicited a strong response in the *Globe Silver Belt* of September 26, following the attempted robbery of a Tombstone stage. A decrease in the number of "loafers" and cowboys would be a public benefit, the paper declared, and Tombstone had many. As Wells Fargo detective James B. Hume remarked to his girlfriend in 1881, "Six thousand population—five thousand are bad—one thousand of them known outlaws." No wonder Wyatt and Morgan Earp rode shotgun for Wells Fargo.

The stage going from Tucson to Tombstone was robbed on the 16th by two Americans who presented shot-guns. The passengers. (seven) were robbed. The mail was not molested. The offenders are supposed to be tramps loafing at Tombstone. Acting Governor Gosper's head was level when he offered a reward for nipping the thread of life of a stage robber. Instead of $500 he should have doubled the sum. The violent death of a road agent is cheap at any price.

Madison Larkin was steady and sober, traits that fitted him to be a Wells Fargo agent and a Prohibition Party presidential hopeful. In 1877, Phoenix agent Larkin resolutely guarded silver bars from the Tip Top Mine. (Courtesy of the Arizona Historical Foundation, Tempe, Arizona.)

Elegant Charles E. Boles tantalized the public starting in the mid-1870s. A disappointed gold-seeker in the 1850s and a Union soldier in the 1860s, Boles turned to a new mode of making money in the 1870s: stagecoach robbing. A dreaded outlaw in an 1871 science-fiction story inspired him to adopt the desperado's name, Black Bart.

REWARD

WELLS, FARGO & CO.'S EXPRESS BOX
on **SONORA AND MILTON STAGE ROUTE, was ROBBED** this morning, near Reynolds' Ferry, by one man, masked and armed with sixteen shooter and double-barreled shot gun. We will pay

$250

for **ARREST and CONVICTION of the Robber.**

San Francisco, July 26, 1875.   JNO. J. VALENTINE, Gen. Supt.

On July 26, 1875, a lone man stopped the stagecoach traveling from gold-rich Tuolumne County to the railhead at Milton. "Throw down the box!" came the command, and the driver complied. An iron safe under the back seat of the stage kept Wells Fargo's losses low. Unfortunately, the losses became all too frequent. This poster commemorates the first. The "sixteen shooter" mentioned is a Henry or Winchester rifle.

This outlaw of eight years was merely misunderstood: He was not a stage robber, but instead a literary man. To his name, "Black Bart," which was taken from Caxton Rhodes's "The Case of Summerfield," Boles added his occupation: "Po8." In an attempt to shorten Black Bart's career, Wells Fargo published the collected works of this minor California poet:

"Here I lay me down to sleep
To wait the coming morrow
Perhaps success, perhaps defeat
And everlasting sorrow
I've labored long and hard for bread
For honor and for riches
But on my corns too long you've tred,
You fine haired sons of bitches
Let come what will, I'll try it on
My condition can't be worse
And if there's money in that Box
Tis munny in my purse."

Black Bart's territory ranged from Calaveras County to southern Oregon, frustrating an endless number of lawmen. At last in 1883, he returned to the scene of his first heist. This time, a hunter with a rifle sent him scurrying away with $5,000 worth of gold, but leaving behind a handkerchief. Its laundry mark, "F.X.0.7.," and the work of many officers finally allowed Wells Fargo detective Jim Hume to crack the case. Released from San Quentin after four years, Black Bart simply disappeared. Pictured from left to right are Sheriff Thomas Cunningham, San Joaquin County; Capt. Appleton W. Stone, San Francisco Police Department; Sheriff Ben Thorn, Calaveras County; detective John W. Thacker, Wells, Fargo & Company; and detective Henry N. Morse.

This 1890 photograph of the Reno staff proved why outlaws should not mess with Wells Fargo. Richmond Smith, agent from 1875 to 1901, stands (fourth from right) with two clerks. Around them are the fierce shotgun messengers who guarded money and treasure on the railroad between San Francisco, Reno, and Ogden. Pictured at far left, scowling, mustachioed San Francisco messenger William W. Fowler particularly did not tolerate fools.

A teenage girl finds shade under an umbrella to escape hot Minnesota sun. Barely more than a wheat station whistle stop on the Chicago, Milwaukee and St. Paul Railway, the Chandler Depot had Wells Fargo and Western Union.

A pair of pet donkeys brought the kids and all the Arkansas cousins together at the Wells Fargo office in Gentry. Blessed with fine soil and good crops, marketing suffered when fruit ripened on the sabbath. In a town divided between Methodists, Baptists, and Seventh-Day Adventists, a suggestion by Wells Fargo agent Elmer Jones brought Gentry together as a community: Methodists and Baptists picked fruit on Saturdays while Adventists worshiped, and Adventists returned the favor on Sundays.

A 20th-century Wells Fargo dogsled brings packages and news to an isolated miner in the far, cold reaches of Alaska.

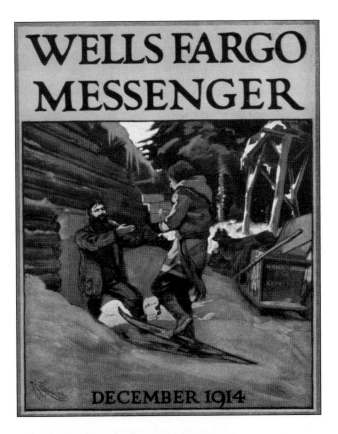

WELLS FARGO MESSENGER

DECEMBER 1914

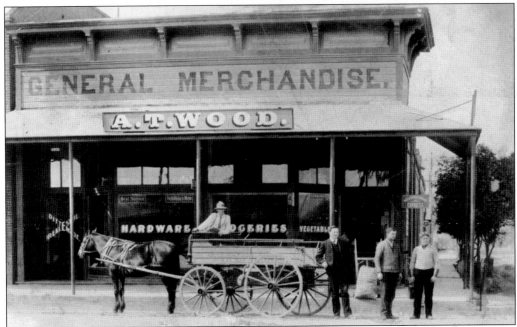

About 1904, Wells Fargo agent Roy L. Acker leans against Wells Fargo's delivery wagon. The driver stands ready to deliver almost anything around Oakdale, California.

Inside the electric-lit Oakdale office about 1904, agent Roy L. Acker stands against the counter, while the back corner features a large Wells Fargo sign. Customers could buy fresh delicacies from display cases on the left and a variety of canned goods from behind the counter. The center barrels held peaches, which one could eat while lying on the sofa cushions advertised above. Acker also sold men's suits, household crockery, and below the counter, framed art.

In 1909, heavy snow in Salem, Oregon, forced Wells Fargo to remove the wheels on its famed delivery wagons and substitute runners. There was no need for the back brakes, either.

About 1908, art deco and mission revival architecture meet in this photograph of the railroad depot in Albuquerque, New Mexico, with 16 Wells Fargo employees standing in front.

In 1909, agent George W. Elder poses in front of his San Francisco district office on 22nd Street, near Valencia Street. Customers could enjoy Wells Fargo convenience without going downtown. Meanwhile, Elder keeps an eye on Dad and Mabel Bentham. Who knows when he might need ostrich feathers curled?

Monterey continues to draw tourists. Now they visit Cannery Row and the Aquarium. Years ago, the lavish Hotel Del Monte drew them in. In 1943, during World War II, the hotel became what is today's Naval Postgraduate School. Of course, souvenirs went home by Wells Fargo.

Hard at work in 1908, William A. Biglow sits in the tidy Antioch office. A large Wells Fargo safe protected money; a Wells Fargo stationery cabinet organized paperwork; and a large map showed where Antioch fit into the Santa Fe Railroad network. "I am here from 8 a.m. until 10 p.m.," a brother agent wrote. "I have made good," but "holy macony, I am *tired*."

At scheduled points heading east and west, Wells Fargo employees cooled down refrigerated rail cars. Large blocks of ice lowered from the roof into cooling compartments at each end of the car regulated temperature. In 1913, Wells Fargo's fleet of 150 refrigerator cars traveled 4.5 million miles, heading to Chicago and New York markets and carrying fish, oysters, dressed poultry, butter, eggs, cream, strawberries, loganberries, raspberries, cherries, grapes, apricots, cantaloupes, asparagus, lettuce, peas, beans, tomatoes, cucumbers, peppers, and spinach.

In Pasadena, Texas, the strawberry growers pictured here bring their crop to Wells Fargo. In 1913, Wells Fargo helped them to inspect, pack, and market 80 carloads of choice fruit. Such was the quality that Eastern buyers bid up the price.

When agriculturalists grew grapes as big as cantaloupes, they sent them by Wells Fargo. Reefers carried seasonal produce across the continent to be the first and freshest in the market.

In late October 1915, Wells Fargo rushed a wagonload of choice large chrysanthemums to New Orleans. Redwood City grower Sadakuso Enomoto, pictured here sitting next to the Wells Fargo driver, knew that thanks to Wells Fargo, his beauties would decorate the tombs of the honored dead on All Saints' Day, November 1.

The Sun-Maid Raisin girl graces a 1918 Wells Fargo wagon banner promoting a Fresno celebration. Wells Fargo specialized in shipping packages of dried California fruits to add vitamin C to eastern diets during the middle of winter.

October 10, 1911, was an auspicious day. Sun Yat-Sen inaugurated the Republic of China, while in Tucson, Arizona, Wells Fargo employee Guy Gwyn (right) helped load 100 bags containing $100,000 in Mexican silver dollars. The three-ton shipment went to China.

Wells Fargo agent Guy Gwyn was the best, bar none. On July 14, 1914, Gwyn dispatched 37 bars of silver from the appropriately named Silver City, New Mexico, to New York. The 3,100 pounds of bullion contained a trace of gold and had a value of 94¢ a troy ounce, which would be about $20 an ounce today. As Wells Fargo had done on Nevada's Comstock 50 years before, Gywn often stacked bars on the sidewalk until he could ship them out. Their average weight of 85 pounds discouraged thieves.

Artist Edward Hopper captured the rhythm and the rush of the express business on a cover of the employee magazine, which depicted friends waving as the express train roars out of a station.

On February 7, 1915, Wells Fargo inaugurated "The Fargo Fast," four days westward from coast to coast. This was "the fastest transcontinental express service that modern railroading can provide," Wells Fargo rightly declared. Connecting with the express train from New York in Chicago, the Santa Fe's "Fargo Fast" reached Los Angeles 13 hours faster and San Francisco 15 hours quicker than had been done previously.

Two women dressed in white pose on a handcar in DeWitt, Missouri, about 1914, when Wells Fargo served 100,000 miles of routes.

I'm sending you something by Wells Fargo Express – *Prepaid* – but you mustn't open it until Christmas

Children rejoiced when Wells Fargo's fast delivery piled gifts under Christmas trees. Naturally, Wells Fargo advertised itself as "The Modern Santa Claus."

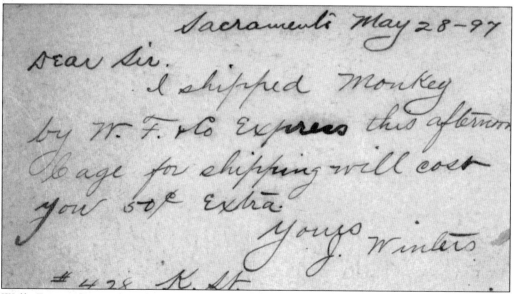

Wells Fargo often engaged in "monkey business"—this time between Sacramento and San Francisco. Similarly, in August 1917, messenger Lavet R. D. Erickson, against all regulations, gave three spider monkeys the joyful run of his express car. Making up for lost time, the train, speeding between Ashland and Portland, sent boxes bouncing, and the monkeys vanished. A forlorn monkeyless messenger searched the train as it pulled into Portland. Cleaning up, he tossed scraps into the stove—and the monkeys popped out and went into their cage. "They look very happy," the delighted owner declared as she tipped the sooty Erickson.

In 1917, Wells Fargo's large San Diego office demanded accurate records. Pictured from left to right, chief clerk Dolly Bodette stands with her staff: Florence Mullineaux, counter clerk; Helen M. Reif, statement clerk; Mrs. Hastings, abstract clerk; and Mrs. Beardsley, office clerk.

Dr. Herman Hollerith played his cards correctly—especially when the government adopted his punch-card-tabulating machines to sort 63 million people in the 1890 census. In 1913, five men sit at electric tabulators in Wells Fargo's Chicago Hollerith bureau, compiling efficiencies and revenues from 8,000 express offices. To the left, a man runs a card-sorter at a rate of over four a second. A key-punch operator "holed" required categories of information or "fields" on three-and-a-half-by-seven-and-three-eighths-inch cards; boxes of these cards surround the room.

Wells Fargo & Co Express

Domestic and Foreign Exchange Department
issues at low rates

── Money Orders ──	── Travelers Checks ──
which can be endorsed from one person to another and used for remittance to all places in the United States, Canada, Mexico and all Countries of the World. Money promptly refunded on lost or stolen orders.	for the safe and convenient use of travelers, at home or abroad. Accepted at par by Hotels, Merchants, and Railroad or Steamship Companies. The signature affixed at time of purchase assures identification.

In 1914, Wells Fargo emphasized its money transfers instead of its package business. Competition from the U.S. Parcel Post, regulation through the Interstate Commerce Commission, and expensive rivalry for railroad contracts cut carrying revenues. In an era without widespread checking accounts or retail-banking offices, Wells Fargo's express offices functioned as branch banks. In 1918, Wells Fargo had 110 offices in Arizona, 900 in California, 60 in Nevada, 130 in New Mexico, 150 in Oregon, and 90 in Washington.

Wells Fargo's blue, red-wheeled wagons were traveling billboards. One early 20th-century poster that adorned wagon sides proclaimed that Wells Fargo's courteous, fast, and efficient service was "The Fargo Way."

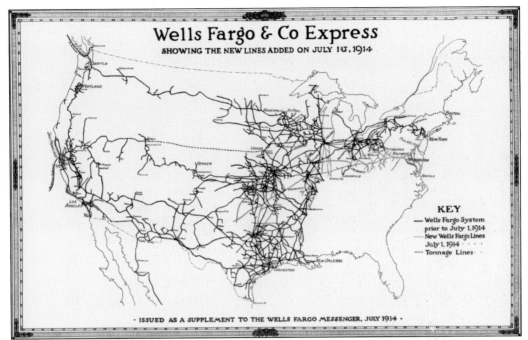

Wells Fargo & Co Express

SHOWING THE NEW LINES ADDED ON JULY 1ST, 1914

KEY
— Wells Fargo System
prior to July 1, 1914
— New Wells Fargo Lines
July 1, 1914 · · · ·
···· Tonnage Lines ·

· ISSUED AS A SUPPLEMENT TO THE WELLS FARGO MESSENGER, JULY 1914 ·

When the U.S. express company elected to go out of business in 1914, the other express companies divided up its rail contracts. Wells Fargo filled in service areas. Blank spots on the map indicate regional monopolies formed by the National Express in New England and the Southern Express within the old Confederacy. Yet each express service attempted to encroach on the other's territory. Within two years, American Express and Adams Express would enter Wells Fargo's California territory. On July 1, 1918, when Wells Fargo joined American Railway Express, it had 10,000 offices nationwide.

World War I killed the best and brightest of Europe. Millions died senselessly in muddy trenches. In 1917, the conflict engulfed the United States, and Wells Fargo did its part. In 1918, in Fargo, North Dakota, Wells Fargo horses protected against the cold haul supplies for the Red Cross, the successor to the Civil War's Sanitary Commission.

In the summer of 1917, a fleet of polished Wells Fargo trucks with matching banners proclaiming "Have Wells Fargo Deliver the Goods" line up at the Baltimore, Maryland, depot. Wells Fargo would outrun the government's parcel post any day. Gas- and electric-powered vehicles pushed Old Dobbin aside in the cities, but horse-drawn vehicles lasted into the 1930s. The Portland office kept its horse-drawn money wagon for years. If robbers struck, they would not get far.

Somewhere in Mexico, Wells Fargo stands ready to help. When the U.S. government nationalized the domestic express business in 1918 during World War I, Wells Fargo continued operations in Mexico.

From 1941 to 1957, ten Wells Fargo stores throughout Mexico sold and financed American agricultural machinery, irrigation pumps, trucks, and spare parts. This one occupies a corner of the Hotel El Paso in Monterrey.

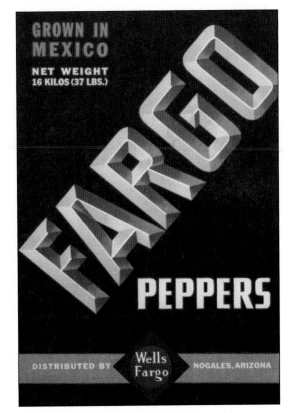

During winter months, Mexican produce fills our grocery-store bins. Wells Fargo was an early shipper of this produce. From 1933 to 1958, it distributed fruits and vegetables from south of the border throughout the United States.

103

In the 1950s, Wells Fargo's express lines radiated out of Havana on the Cuban railroads.

About 1910, clerk William T. Wallup stands ready to serve inside Herman A. Dickel's Anaheim grocery store and Wells Fargo agency. "At Dickel's Grocery," it advertised, "Your wants will all be supplied with the best and freshest line of goods on the market." Wallup, with telephone, directory, date-stamper, and balance scale, produced that quality for Wells Fargo. "Service is the very backbone of the express," Wells Fargo said. "We have very little else to sell in our business. Our merchandise is courtesy, willingness, human ability." These appropriate remarks close Wells Fargo's story of the express business. (Courtesy of First American Title Insurance Company, Santa Ana, California.)

Six

BANKING MATURITY

In the 1860s, settled agricultural Californians replaced roving miners. Manufacturing, farming, and hardrock gold extraction needed long-term capital, and California law changed to permit commercial banks. Wells Fargo changed, too. At the start of this decade, bankers, such as Wells Fargo's Gerritt Bell, were gold assayers; in the 1870s, bankers became, as did Wells Fargo's Homer King, stock experts. Wells Fargo, with banking houses in the major financial centers of San Francisco, California; Carson City and Virginia City, Nevada; Salt Lake City, Utah; and New York City, New York stood ready to aid investment.

Also in the 1860s, the national bank system joined state banks, expanding throughout the West. They further increased the money supply by issuing banknotes carrying their own names. In 1905, due to a charter change, Wells Fargo Nevada National Bank issued such money. As checks became common, criminals creatively made forged and altered financial paper a growth industry.

The financial panics of 1893 and 1907 battered banks and crippled consumers. Without any insurance for depositors, customers lost all when a bank closed. Additionally, the 1906 San Francisco earthquake disrupted financial institutions in the commercial center of the Pacific coast. Better-regulated national banks gained prestige, and California's oldest banks converted to national charters. All built magnificent "banking temples" that gave outward appearance of permanence.

In 1909, as California's urban centers grew, the legislature led the nation with a new banking act that allowed one institution to have commercial, savings, and trust departments, rather than have investors establish separate institutions. As sunny Southern California attracted immigrants and the Great War brought more women into the work force, retail banking grew. One bank could offer all departmental services through its branch banks, often in different cities.

The Federal Reserve System began on November 16, 1914, to manage the country's money supply. Additionally, it set up a check-clearing system that allowed any bank check to be cashed anywhere in the country. Banks came to offer customers the financial services that Wells Fargo & Company Express had provided. Between 1920 and 1930, branch banks grew from one-fifth to two-thirds of all banking offices in California.

Wells Fargo president Frederick L. Lipman spoke for those institutions offering wholesale banking for large commercial clients. They preferred to do business with other independent, responsible, and professional out-of-town bankers who developed strong "personal relationships with customers."

On January 1, 1924, Wells Fargo joined with the Union Trust Company, the pioneer corporate trustee on the Pacific coast, founded in 1893 under a more flexible state charter. Conservative management since 1852 enabled Wells Fargo Bank to weather all financial crises, even before the protective Federal Deposit Insurance Corporation went into operation in 1934.

The Great Depression was no different. President Lipman assured the board that Wells Fargo was "actually earning" its dividend, and the bank continued to pay it. "We shall function as usual," he announced, "meeting all demands under any circumstances."

World War II united the country, and when the troops went off to fight, women entered the work force in unprecedented numbers. With their help, shipbuilders, airplane fabricators, and manufacturers met huge, rapid, wartime production goals.

In the late 1940s, Wells Fargo faced dramatically altered postwar demographics. A growing customer base clamored to purchase automobiles and homes, while the invention of the transistor and silicon chip promised to handle immensely increasing paperwork through electronic data processing. Frederick Lipman, though, held his course for unit banking.

In 1960, Wells Fargo and American Trust Company joined, the latter supplying 102 Northern California branches, making a total of 113. Two years later, the bank adopted a distinctive stagecoach logo, and in 1964, introduced Californians to award-winning scenic checks—with a stagecoach design, of course. Indispensable consumer credit came in 1967, when Wells Fargo offered Master Charge—now MasterCard—credit cards.

In the mid-1970s, the Crocker Bank led California banks in the widespread use of automated teller machines (ATMs). By the early 1980s, they were ubiquitous. The 1980s brought deregulation, high interest rates (the prime rate was 20.5 percent in 1981), the collapse of the savings-and-loan industry, intense foreign-banking competition, gradual interstate banking, and an uncertain market. Wells Fargo turned to electronics and the Internet for solutions and to plan for the future.

At the same time, Wells Fargo grew greatly. On May 30, 1986, Wells Fargo doubled in size through the purchase of Crocker Bank. Another doubling came on April 1, 1996, with the First Interstate acquisition that made Wells Fargo an interstate bank again.

The next doubling came on November 2, 1998, through a merger with the Norwest Bank of Minneapolis. Now the 160,000 Wells Fargo employees offer banking in 23 states, mortgage and financial services throughout the nation, as well as banking on the Internet.

Drawing on a century and a half of quality, CEO Richard Kovacevich phrased Wells Fargo's mission this way: "We want to satisfy all of our customers' financial needs [and] help them succeed financially." The esprit de corps of express days is apparent, as Wells Fargo continues to be "a company that believes in people as a competitive advantage, a great place to work, [and] an employer of choice."

As the 1860s began, the incredibly rich silver mines of Nevada's Comstock Lode paid huge dividends—but required equally large sums to extract the bullion. Speculation ran rampant. In Gold Hill, Nevada Territory, ore wagons load in front of the Yellow Jacket, Kentuck, Confidence, Challenge, Empire, and Imperial Mines.

African American lithographer Grafton Tyler Brown designed a beautiful stock certificate for the Wells Fargo Mining Company. Without strong trademark laws, it appropriated the Wells Fargo name. Furthermore, although it had no connection with Wells, Fargo & Company, the mine had Brown draw the symbol of universal Wells Fargo service, the stagecoach. The fine graphics, however, are all investors received. The company "mined" stockholders by charging assessments, and it produced no bullion.

Comstock miners bored and burrowed through barren borrasca, seeking rich bonanza ore and leaving a honeycomb of deteriorating tunnels and square-timbered vaults underneath Virginia City, Nevada. By 1930, settling ground made Wells Fargo's grand office a ruin.

The interior of the now-vanished Wells Fargo banking and express office in Virginia City, Nevada, displays the company's services. The "Stocks Bought and Sold" sign reflects the speculative mining economy.

Between 1865 and 1906, Thomas Selby's frame shot-making tower loomed 200 feet over San Francisco as an industrial symbol. Beginning in the 1870s, Selby refined more gold and silver than the U.S. mint. Around it, at First and Howard Streets, clustered numerous iron foundries, which manufactured the mining machinery used throughout the West.

"Loans made on approved Securities," reads this 1870 advertisement. President Lloyd Tevis and company secretary Homer S. King changed Wells Fargo from gold-dust-buying-based banking to entrepreneurial, loan-making, commercial banking.

From 1876 to 1891, Wells, Fargo & Company's Bank resided at the northeast corner of California and Sansome Streets in a cast-iron building designed by George Gordon. In 1870, the inquisitive Gordon, who created a sugar refinery and a lavish residential community at South Park, turned to earthquake protection. The plank foundation and iron-braced inner wooden structure gave this building flexibility. This stout 45-by-90-foot building survived the huge 1906 earthquake, only to be devoured by the following fire. In 1878, Wells Fargo was the only commercial bank with a telephone; ten years later, a lattice of wires connects telephones and district telegraphs. Inside, large vaults occupied the eastern wall, laurel inlay set off the elegant black walnut furnishings, and two large revolvers hung under the counter.

This interior view of the London and San Francisco Bank on March 19, 1887, resembles Wells Fargo's similarly arranged facilities a block away. Swivel electric lights illuminate fashionable black walnut furniture and fixtures. Tellers met customers along the wide counters, which allowed them to easily scoop stacks of gold coins. High slanted desks and a long row of rubber stamps facilitated paper pushing.

In the 20th century, American Trust Company (Wells Fargo's 1960 merger partner) used the London and San Francisco Bank's ornate 1873 cast-iron building on the northwest corner of California and Leidesdorff Streets. The long banking counter stretched along the 97-foot Leidesdorff side. Three ornate 14-foot vaults reposed on the main floor; two vaults for Mexican, trade, and standard silver dollars occupied the basement.

Wells Fargo's current headquarters stands on this 1873 banking location. The Fulton Iron Foundry's cast-iron hitching post reminds pedestrians of earlier days.

In 1888, the Nevada Bank (left), at the northwest corner of Montgomery and Pine Streets, equaled the ornate lavishness of its neighbors. Conveniently across the street is the main Western Union Telegraph Office. In 1897, the Nevada Bank became a national bank, and on April 24, 1905, through a merger, the Wells Fargo Nevada National Bank.

For 50 years, San Francisco banks shoved gold coins across open counters. In the 1890s, they adopted Eastern methods, where paper was the circulating money. This photograph shows ornamental brass grills and opaque glass-caged tellers in Wells Fargo's 1890s location on Market Street. Ceiling-tall partitions enclosed bank officers. Radiators provided steam heat, while brass foot rails gave a cozy saloon feeling.

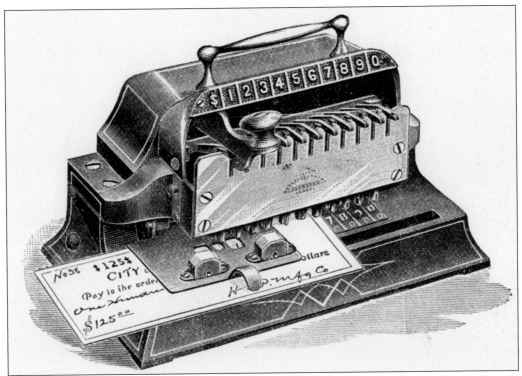

To combat the extensive "white collar" crime of check forgery, the late 19th century saw the rise of safety paper that could not be chemically altered and the invention of numerous machines that cut or punched numerals through the paper to make them impossible to change.

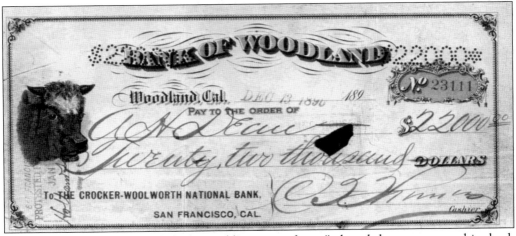

In 1895, Herman Becker, called "the world's greatest forger," altered the amount on this check from $12 to $22,000, the record for a "raised" check. He claimed to have punched numbers with a darning needle, as possession of a check protector would have automatically proven guilt. Comparison of the dot-made numerals reveals he did use one. A special magnifying camera proved the forgery and sent Becker to San Quentin for seven and a half years.

When Wells, Fargo & Company's Bank joined Isaias W. Hellman's Nevada National Bank on April 24, 1905, the combined bank continued under a national charter. National banks, with the prestige of the federal government backing them, gained great advertising when an 1863 law allowed them to issue money displaying their name and charter number. The $10 bill pictured here carries the signature of Vice President Frederick L. Lipman, who dominated Wells Fargo for a half century.

Bavarian-born Isaias W. Hellman (1842–1920) immigrated to Los Angeles and, in the mid-1860s, founded the then-sleepy town's first bank. In 1890, Hellman moved north to rescue the Nevada Bank of San Francisco. In 1893, Hellman formed the first corporate trustee on the Pacific coast, the Union Trust Company, and the first Italian bank, the Columbus Savings and Loan Society. As president of the Wells Fargo Nevada National Bank (1905–1920), Hellman stated philosophically, "Our ambition is not to be the largest bank in San Francisco, but to be the soundest and the best."

On the morning of April 18, 1906, cashier Frederick Lipman woke up at 5:12 a.m. with a shock, as his Oakland house shook and chimneys tumbled down around him. Just offshore from Golden Gate Park, the San Andreas Fault slipped in an earthquake estimated at 7.9 on the Richter scale. As he did ordinarily, Lipman took a ferry that deposited him at the Ferry Building at the foot of California Street. To his left, buildings blazed along Market Street, but Lipman continued on to work at the bank.

At 9:00 a.m., as usual, the Wells Fargo Nevada National Bank at Montgomery and Pine Streets opened. Except for rubble in the streets and excitement, everything went on normally. At 10:30 a.m., firemen chased out the bankers, and Lipman, after taking his father's pocket watch from a drawer, took the ferry home. He did not go to the opera that night as planned.

INTERIOR VIEW OF THE NEVADA BANK.

About 4:00 p.m., the ravenous fire reached the bay side of Montgomery Street. As this view from the Fairmont Hotel shows, the two center buildings, the Kohl Building on Montgomery at California Streets and the Merchants Exchange at 465 California Street, remain untouched. Both buildings still stand, and Wells Fargo's head office adjoins the Kohl Building. About 4:30 p.m., raging flames crossed Montgomery Street and the Nevada Block, at the northwest corner with Pine Street, was no more. Soon Lipman telegraphed: "Building Destroyed. Vaults Intact. Our Position Unimpaired."

Neither earthquake nor fire would stop Wells Fargo's banking. On Monday, April 23, 1906, the bank opened in the home of Emanuel S. Heller, President Isaias W. Hellman's son-in-law, above the Van Ness Avenue firebreak. At 2020 Jackson Street, Wells Fargo shared quarters with Hellman's Union Trust Company and the law firm of Heller, Powers & Company. Sitting around the dining room table, Wells Fargo employees conducted business with whatever stationery was handy—including elementary school composition books.

Downtown at Montgomery and Pine Streets, bank employees guarded the hot vaults at night. Four guards spent two weeks, standing two shifts, 8:00 p.m. to 2:00 a.m., and 2:00 a.m. to 8:00 a.m. The great St. Louis fire of 1849 taught the lesson that fireproof vaults opened too soon would allow a fresh supply of oxygen to ignite superheated paper.

On May 1, a temporary Clearing House Bank opened in the U.S. mint at Fifth and Mission Streets. Walter McGavin, Wells Fargo's Assistant Cashier, ran the show. Each bank had a representative to accept deposits and cash checks under $500—but only after the bank's temporary office had approved the check. With records in the cooling vaults, bankers relied on memories—and Lipman possessed a superb one. "I don't think we lost $200 in paying out thousands," he said.

Workmen hammer at steel doors to discover that fireproof vaults lived up to expectations. Wells Fargo lost only one ledger, covering a portion of the alphabet, but its footings, the added accounts at the very bottom, were intact. Working with deposit slips and other records, Wells Fargo recreated what had been burnt.

With policemen on guard, employees remove sacks of gold coin from the vaults of the Wells Fargo Nevada National Bank.

On May 21, 1906, Wells Fargo Bank moved into the lightly damaged 1895 Union Trust Company Building at Market and Montgomery Streets. From here, President Frederick Lipman defended unit banking against the spreading fervor of branch banking. In a 1923 address, "The Relations of the City Banks with their Country Correspondents," Lipman argued for a relationship between equals, rather than a superior head office making decisions for inferior branches. Wells Fargo remained here until 1960.

Three imposingly secure "banking temples" stood at "Bankers' Corner" in 1911. The camera looks from Market Street towards Post and Montgomery Streets. The buildings are, at left, the Crocker National Bank (1892); center, the First National Bank (1908); and at right, the Wells Fargo Nevada National Bank (1895). Today only the First National Bank building at 1 Montgomery Street survives as a Wells Fargo branch. A rooftop garden replaced the top 10 floors.

Customers flooded the lobby of the Wells Fargo Nevada National Bank on Saturday, August 11, 1923. On July 16, 1917, during World War I, banks began to settle interbank accounts with paper transfers at the Federal Reserve Bank, and gold quickly vanished from circulation. Californians finally accepted paper money.

During World War I, the Northwestern National Bank brass band enlivened morale with patriotic tunes. Wells Fargo's William Fargo helped found this Minneapolis bank in 1872. The family tie grew in 1998 through a Wells Fargo–Norwest merger. (Northwest Bancorporation Collection, Courtesy of the Minnesota Historical Society.)

"We do not know what the future will bring forth," bank president Frederick Lipman observed. "We do, however, know that the future will bring the unexpected, and the unexpected will generally be unfavorable." Not all shared in the prosperity of the 1920s, and the government instituted special loans for veterans of World War I. Times got much worse before they began to get better.

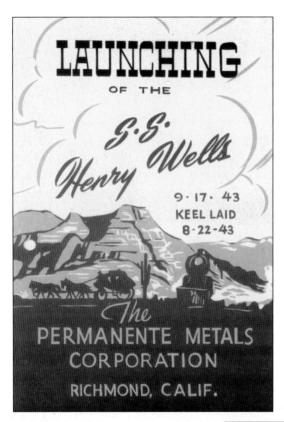

LAUNCHING
OF THE
S.S.
Henry Wells
9·17·43
KEEL LAID
8·22·43
The
PERMANENTE METALS
CORPORATION
RICHMOND, CALIF.

During World War II, African Americans left the South for San Francisco Bay Area shipyards. Workers produced the hundreds of merchant ships that brought supplies to the boys on distant South Seas islands. Most famous were the simply designed, prefabricated, sturdily made, 441-foot Liberty Ships, represented today by the *Jeremiah O'Brien*, berthed in San Francisco.

Less than a month after laying the keel, the *Henry Wells* slid down the ways. The yard delivered the ship on September 26, 1943. In Los Angeles, California Ship Building took slightly longer to start (March 2, 1943), launch (March 29), and deliver (April 12) the *William G. Fargo*.

As wartime shortages turned to memories in the 1950s, banks mobilized to meet the multitude of Americans driving cars. The Des Moines National Bank, a member of the Norwest family, provided smiling evening service to Iowans. (Courtesy of the Minnesota Historical Society, Northwest Bancorporation Collection.)

Wells Fargo's 1960 partner, the American Trust Company, brought a broad retail-banking network of 102 offices. One was the South Berkeley branch, a 1906 building at 3290 Adeline Street. American Trust was the second oldest bank in California, emerging from the first savings-and-loan institution. The San Francisco Accumulating Fund of 1854 gave women full rights, introduced installment loans, and enabled settlers to purchase homesteads and houses.

Wells Fargo's computer-punch-card operations center in 1965 shows little change from the express company's Hollerith Bureau 50 years previously.

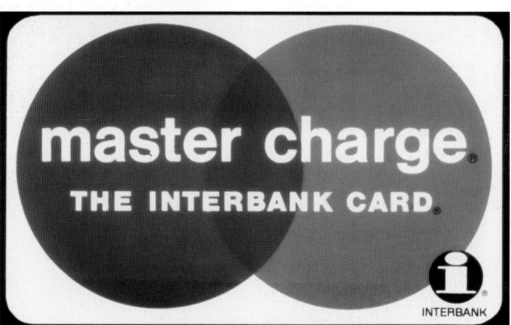

In 1967, Wells Fargo joined with three banks to launch the Master Charge consumer credit card (MasterCard since 1979), ushering in an era of easier borrowing. Within six months, 80 banks offered it, and acceptance surpassed all expectations.

Colonel George Spencer "Spanky" Roberts flew 78 combat missions during World War II and commanded the 99th Fighter Squadron in the North African and Italian campaigns. In 1968, Colonel Roberts brought the skills he gained as a pioneer Tuskegee Airman to become a Wells Fargo credit officer in Sacramento. (Courtesy of Edith Roberts.)

In 1970, Wells Fargo Bank began a pilot Automated Teller Machine program in San Diego. Customers used a specially encoded Master Charge credit card at three locations to make withdrawals. In the mid-1970s, Crocker Bank led the major California banks in the installation of ATMs. In the early 1980s, ATMs became ubiquitous and indispensable.

The Crocker Bank, which Wells Fargo acquired in 1986, had a split personality. Its founding date of 1870 came from the First National Gold Bank of San Francisco, the first national bank in California. Railroad magnate Charles Crocker organized Crocker-Woolworth & Company in 1883, and it contributed the name. The two joined heritages in 1926 and kept both. A cuddly playful pun, the well-remembered "Crocker Spaniel" went in 1979 to customers who made deposits of $300 or more. This merger doubled Wells Fargo's size within California.

Amadeo Peter Giannini knew California commerce from years as a produce buyer and became the state's leading promoter of branch banking. Within California, Giannini worked through his 1904 Bank of Italy/America. To manage out-of-state banks, he used his 1928 Transamerica Corporation, whose banking business evolved into First Interstate Bank. Wells Fargo purchased First Interstate Bank in 1996, making the oldest banks in Arizona, Colorado, Oregon, and Utah part of the Wells Fargo family.

A. P. GIANNINI
THE
BANKAMERICAN

Wells Fargo's History Museum, one of nine, welcomes visitors to the corporate headquarters at 420 Montgomery Street, virtually on the spot where Wells Fargo opened in 1852. Since 1935, Wells Fargo Bank's history program has invited tourists inside, conducted school tours, and assisted researchers to share a rich history. (Courtesy of Michael Wakeman.)

ACROSS AMERICA, PEOPLE ARE DISCOVERING SOMETHING WONDERFUL. *THEIR HERITAGE.*

Arcadia Publishing is the leading local history publisher in the United States. With more than 3,000 titles in print and hundreds of new titles released every year, Arcadia has extensive specialized experience chronicling the history of communities and celebrating America's hidden stories, bringing to life the people, places, and events from the past. To discover the history of other communities across the nation, please visit:

www.arcadiapublishing.com

Customized search tools allow you to find regional history books about the town where you grew up, the cities where your friends and family live, the town where your parents met, or even that retirement spot you've been dreaming about.